Here,
Now,
With You

D0596893

Gregg Louis Taylor

Here
Now
With You

Six Movements of Compassion for Life and Leadership

🔁) Abingdon Press™

Nashville

HERE, NOW, WITH YOU:
SIX MOVEMENTS OF COMPASSION FOR LIFE AND LEADERSHIP

Copyright © 2019 by Gregg Louis Taylor

This book is printed on acid-free paper.

Library of Congress Cataloging-in-Publication Data has been requested.

978-1-5018-6817-7

Scripture quotations are taken from the Common English Bible, copyright 2011. Used by permission. All rights reserved.

19 20 21 22 23 24 25 26 27 28 29—10 9 8 7 6 5 4 3 2 1

MANUFACTURED IN THE UNITED STATES OF AMERICA

Contents

Foreword

A gang member I know tells me that "the minute my feet touch the floor every morning," he's "on the lookout." I ask what he's looking for. "God, of course." Of course. We are not just searching for signs of the Divine or a sacramental rhyming with our Creator's creative impulses. We want to align our hearts to the tender glance of God, and then, once our feet hit the floor, we choose to be that tender glance in the world. We want to inhabit more fully the spacious and expansive compassion of God. As a lifer at Folsom prison once said to me, "Compassion IS God." We are on the lookout for not just THIS God but for ways to be THIS God in the world.

The great Gregg Louis Taylor, in this book, helps us put one compassionate foot in front of the next. As we reflect on the arc of the six movements Gregg helpfully and practically presents to us, we find ourselves reintroduced to the joy of being "compassionate as God is compassionate." What we once thought of as the grim duty of the highly compassionate person becomes the lavish and abundant joy we have access to in compassion. It is no longer an invitation to share and pass over into the pain and suffering of others but a gracious upending of our own notions of the root of all happiness. We foster and nurture a praxis of compassion, not because it's the harder thing but because it is the gentle pathway to an open, tender heart. And once we are no longer a stranger to that heart, we know what Jesus wants to give us: "My joy yours...your joy complete."

A homie, who works at Homeboy Industries, and his wife walk their four-year-old son to his first day of school. They stand and wave, and the little guy is led into the building by his teacher. The parents wave until their kid disappears into the school. As they turn to walk to the car, the homie begins to sob, and his wife is startled by the outburst. "He's gonna be ok," she said, flummoxed by her mate's emotions. "I mean, why are you crying?"

When he can speak, he says, "When I was a kid, we didn't have glasses or cups. We drank out of old pickle jars. We didn't know what silverware was. We'd jack ketchup packets from McDonald's and call it lunch. And we wiped our asses with newspaper." He composes himself a bit and points back to the building where his son has just entered. "And now," he continues, "my son just walked into school wearing new clothes and carrying a brand-new backpack." He settles into the truth of this. "*That's* why I'm crying."

God is dropping us hints as to where our treasures are hidden. And at the same time, we feel more at home in our connection to each other and in the gift of our shared humanity. Then we rest in the stillness of love—and choose to love the stillness of God.

Gregg takes us on a rich journey that reminds us all of our unshakable goodness and comforts us as we choose the praxis of tenderness, the compassionate heart that reveals to us all our true selves in loving. Gregg teaches us to lead in the best way, by fanning the flames of tenderness, until all hearts are open to our own compassionate truth. And what a joy to be in this together.

Gregory Boyle
Founder of Homeboy Industries
Author of *Tattoos on the Heart: The Power of Boundless Compassion* and *Barking to the Choir: The Power of Radical Kinship*

Acknowledgments

Since I am quite sure this book would not exist if left to my own devices, you are reading these words because a number of people have pushed, prodded, and paved the way to make this project happen.

I think of my longtime friend Richard Gandy. For as long as I can remember, he has encouraged me to write, mainly by poking me with the gentle, encouraging (and sometimes nagging) question, "Are you writing anything?" Thank you, brother. Is now the time when you stop renting space in my head?

I am deeply grateful to the good folks at Abingdon for the opportunity. You work tirelessly behind the scenes to make sure people like me don't mess things up—or at least you significantly decrease the chances. Thank you, Connie Stella. Your patience, guidance, and wisdom kept me from getting lost in the weeds, and when I did, you pulled me out to ensure I spent limited time there.

To my more-supportive-than-a-man-deserves wife, who read my ramblings and, without regard for my ego, offered necessary insight and wise feedback while graciously affording me the time and space to write—even when that meant not showing up at the dinner table because I was busy staring at a blinking cursor on a screen. Thank you, Amy, for making room and for making this book better.

To the Houston reVision community, which models each day what improbable friendships and transformative kindness can look like, it's a joy to be among you.

Acknowledgments

Finally, to all those who have been patient to walk with me over the years and continue to allow me to accompany them as we try to make sense of living and loving on this long-haul journey to compassion-*ate* our world, everything I know I have learned from you. Thank you for opening yourselves to me with generosity and spaciousness. You're the real reason this book exists.

Introduction

You may be picking up this book because you find yourself stuck in a spiritual journey, mired down from going through the religious motions, stymied by a spirituality gone stale. And yet you suspect there is more—much more. You're looking to increase the bandwidth of divine connection, to experience a fuller expression of what it means to be you, to engage meaningfully in the relationships interfacing with your world. Maybe the church and organized religion have burned you, or you have carried far too long a saved-by-grace-but-live-by-guilt spirituality, and said to yourself and others, "No more! I'm out!" Nevertheless, although skepticism remains, something tells you that to entirely shut the door on this God thing would be to close the door on yourself.

You may have come to this book because you're a pastor or church staff member, a volunteer leader in a congregation or a facilitator in a small group. It's likely that many folks you seek to lead are in situations similar to those mentioned above. As a leader, what you want more than anything is to cultivate a wildly welcoming, compassionate space of grace in which anyone connected to or touched by your community feels accepted and loved. You're curious about how compassion can become a conduit for conscious contact with the presence of God. You're looking to inspire your congregation to get out of the seats and into the streets. You long to lead your people to be the church, actively engaged in the issues and challenges of your broader community, committed to justice and to the restoration of all that is unjust.

Of course, you could have grabbed this book for a thousand and one other reasons. Whoever you are, wherever you're coming from, and whatever you're carrying, I'm glad you're here. Welcome to what I hope will be the beginning or a continuation of a quest for a compassion-filled life that enriches your conscious contact with God and expands the ways you relate to your internal and external worlds. The pages ahead are written with you in mind.

"Be compassionate just as God is compassionate"—Jesus's words, not mine—is an invitation to a journey of cultivating compassion-filled lives and leadership. Along the way, we experience conscious contact with God and authentic connection with one another by paying attention to compassion's movement in all of life.

With that in mind, two questions shape the contents of this book: What does compassion's movement look like in our lives? How can we cultivate it once aware? In other words, what experiences open the door to recognizing compassion? And rather than ignore or resist them when they occur, how can we pay attention to what's happening and further cultivate rich expressions of compassion in life and leadership?

Beginning with the prologue, part 1, "Considering Compassion," takes a look at six ways we experience compassion's movement in our lives. Each chapter reflects on one of those six in the context of experiences, stories, and relational interactions. In some cases, for reasons of confidentiality, I've changed the names of people included in the stories. Without taking away from the integrity of the stories, some details have been omitted or changed for the same reason.

Although part 1 is written to stand on its own, I hope that you will want to dig a little deeper in part 2, "Conversations and Cultivations." Each chapter in part 2 has a parallel in part 1. The content is designed to be reflective, interactive, and application-oriented without telling you exactly what to do. There's plenty of room in the process for input.

Anyone can use part 2 for meaningful conversations and worthwhile practices to further cultivate compassion. The five-step process for groups (meaning more than one person) will help you to *Recap, Reflect on, Respond to,* and *Re-engage* each respective movement of compassion I've written about in part 1, as well as help you prepare to *Return* to the next session. To maximize the flow of the content, I suggest reading a chapter in part 1 and then turning to its parallel in part 2 for conversations and cultivations. Move to the next chapter in part 1, and so on.

Of course, the entire book can be read individually, but since compassion is experienced and cultivated only in and through relationships, reading and reflecting on it in the company of others will provide a richer, more interesting, shared journey with the potential to catalyze collective change. You may have a staff or a team you are leading, a small group or book club you are involved with, or a friend or two with similar stirrings about what a compassion-filled life could look like. Invite some folks into the conversation. As far as I can tell, God has a way of showing up when two or three gather together.

PART ONE | CONSIDERING COMPASSION

Conscious Contact

W hat's past is prologue, wrote Shakespeare. I suppose he's on to something. Not in the sense that past conditions or choices set us on a predetermined course toward inescapable outcomes, but more in the way a story unfolds new meaning with each telling. There are moments in the past that somehow transcend the passage of time to mold the present and create momentum for the future. They leave a mark. Imprinted in the soul, such moments are anchor and sail—holding us in being, releasing us to catch the wind of becoming. At least that's my experience.

Not even close to ripe, I was green. More like raw in the role of "pastor" when I walked into a hospital room to meet a forty-eight-year-old woman named Alma. She had been involved in a traffic accident, hit by a drunk driver. That's all the information I had been given. Tapping lightly on the door, I cracked it open to make sure the way was clear. She sat in a recliner next to the bed wearing a halo brace, a medieval-looking contraption of metal rods extending upward out of a stiff plastic vest strapped around her torso, bolted to a metal ring screwed into her skull. Bruises, slashes, and wounds covered her arms, legs, and face; her bottom lip puffed up like she'd gone a few rounds in the ring. After I introduced myself, she welcomed me in, motioned to an empty chair, and extended an invitation to join her. As soon as I sat down, Alma took my right hand, held it gently, and began talking, squeezing my palm and fingers almost rhythmically to the beat of her story. She spoke about the usual stuff: family, work, where she was from, plans for the future, and whatever details she could remember about the collision that had landed her in this room with a broken neck and a barely broken-in pastor.

A little while later, I suggested we pray. After the amen part, I began my exit strategy. I opened the door and turned to wish her well when she said something that penetrated the professional distance and detachment they say pastors are supposed to carry in these kinds of situations. "I knew you'd come," she said and then waited for silence to soak the space between us. "God always makes his presence known."

I didn't know if it was what she said or the love or light or something else that seemed to pour through her to fill the room as she said it (probably a combo), but immediately I became unsettled. Within me, in a place I don't remember ever having gained access to, something stirred, even shifted. My face flushed. Seemingly well-hidden, adult-son-of-an-alcoholic insecurity, self-doubt, and baked-in shame flared up. I stood frozen, dumbfounded, no idea how to respond as the moment took on more and more...what? Weightiness? Thickness? I felt awkward. She did not. To extricate myself, the only words I could think to stutter were "Thank you," but they came out sounding more like a question—"Thank you?"

I rushed out of Alma's room extremely uncomfortable in my own skin, hurried down long, sanitized hallways, passing nurses' stations, medical carts, gurneys, men and women wearing white coats and stethoscopes. With each step her words banged around inside my head, over and over again like they were knocking on the door to my heart: *I knew you'd come. God always makes his presence known. I knew you'd come. God always makes his presence known.* How do you make sense of such encounters, where something divine stirs the deep waters of your humanness to reveal what you do not or cannot yet see, and invites you to a wholeness of life you have not yet known?[1] I couldn't get her words out of my head. *What does that mean?* Like happening upon a burning bush unconsumed by the fire, I was sure that something of God's presence was happening in her. For her to suggest that God's presence was made known in *me*, well, that was jarring.

Spotting a chair in the lobby behind a column, I sat down and sweated. I began thinking or praying or contemplating or something. Somewhere in the moments that followed, Alma's words transitioned to a restless prayer within me. *What does that mean, Lord? You mean that you make your presence known in me?* Building a case for why this could not be true, all I heard was

4

the rambling litany of self-diminishing, automatic negative thoughts that, for as long as I could remember, played like an auto-repeat soundtrack in my head: *Insecure, afraid of failing, anxious about succeeding, not up to the task, not faithful enough, committed enough, smart enough, loving enough, Christian enough, obedient enough, holy enough, never measuring up, colossal disappointment… oh, and let's not forget… vertically challenged, me! You make your presence known in me?*

And then something happened. I didn't hear it with my ears. It didn't seem to come from my brain. It wasn't outside me; it wasn't a thought in me. I'm not exactly sure from where the whisper came, but reverberating through me, thoroughly, I felt the sound: *Yes! I make my presence known in you.*

It's been over thirty years since unplanned providence thought it a good idea to introduce me to Alma and, through her, conscious contact with something divine. Her words still sound in my soul. I suspect they always will. She gave me a theological education worth more than all the years and money I spent on a master of divinity degree (a credential that, it seems to me, overreaches a bit). I'm still a pastor—mainly due to her, I think. But more than a pastor, a person still trying to make meaning of words of God spoken through the fractured body of a beautiful African American woman with a broken neck and a halo bolted to her head.

Many "Almas" along the way have generously shared their lives with me and invited me to share mine with them. Most have no academic degrees hanging on a wall, letters behind their names, or "credentials" to claim. In whatever ministry context I've found myself—from major urban environments to outlying rural areas, university campuses to maximum-security prisons, stripped-down rooms of AA, NA, and many other *A*s to well-adorned sanctuaries of big-steeple churches—a whole host of characters on a sliding scale of sanity have been my companions. Younger and older, they've come from diverse backgrounds, experiences, and ethnicities, back alleys and suburban neighborhoods, varied religious or irreligious perspectives—churched, nonchurched or dechurched, believers and atheists and everything in between. Together we've been on a quest, seeking answers to questions familiar to us all. Questions about the past, present, and future; faith, hope, and love; doubt, despair, and disconnection; why things are the way they are and what it might be like if things were different. And, of course, the biggie—what about this God thing? The truth is, everything I've been able to discern thus far about any of this, I've learned from them. They have been (and continue to be) my spiritual directors, theological mentors, my professors of personhood.

So I guess when it comes down to it, my life and work have always been about leaning in and learning to communicate what occurred in a hospital room over thirty years ago. How does God make conscious contact with us? Suspending for the moment intellectualized answers that tend to get stuck in the head, doctrinal statements that don't necessarily translate to real-life concerns, or sappy, overspiritualized bumper sticker responses to complex, painful experiences ("Just have faith!"), exactly how does God's God-ness meet us on the shaky ground of our being-human-ness? What does willingness to come into one another's orbit have to do with it? Is there something both within us and within the heart of God that connects us all together? If so, what is it and how is it cultivated?

The pages ahead are about something as common to being human as the heart beating inside your chest. You come ready-made with it direct from the manufacturer. You know what it is to experience it; you know what it is to resist it.

Always accessible, it is not readily expressed. Your capacity to access and express it can be diminished by the awful things you have experienced. Yet the terrible things you've been through can open your life to it in ways that make you think, *Maybe this is what it means to be human; maybe this is what it feels like to encounter God.*

Your willingness to apply it to yourself takes you to the freeing space of self-awareness and self-acceptance. Learning to love yourself, you find God in yourself and yourself in God amid the messy mix of your own humanness.

With it, churches, ministries, and even organizations flourish with a felt, life-giving sense of authenticity, grace, and hope. Without it, they become chilled, stagnant, disconnected, and even downright mean.

With it comes God's gift of experiencing what it means to be loved and to love in the ways Jesus knew his own belovedness and showed others theirs. It centered him, nourishing and birthing his life from within the loving, creative space of the womb of Yahweh. It inspired his imagination to see the world God dreams, to see the world as others see it, and to help others appreciate what God has in mind for them.

It moved Jesus inward toward that sacred, albeit sometimes scary space of touching his own pain and coming to grips with his own identity. With visceral stirring in his gut, it compelled him outward to stand and to suffer with others; fighting for those who could not fight for themselves, embracing with tenderness folks not only trying to survive on the margins of society but struggling to find meaning in the anguishing throes of dehumanizing hopelessness.

It is something divine. It is something human. It is where the divine and human meet. That something is compassion.

"Be compassionate just as your Father is compassionate," Jesus echoes Torah, hoping someone might catch wind of who God is and the universal cosmic kindness by which God always shows up.[2] Audaciously, he takes it a step further, suggesting that God's compassionating presence loves to make personal appearances, pinpointing that the spirituality of compassion locates itself in the physicality of relationships. In other words, compassion has skin on it and compels us to have skin in the game. Your skin. My skin. Our skin… in the game. The presence of God is made known through the presence of women, men, and children. People like you and me—who, because of (not despite) their own pain and brokenness, step out with courage to expand capacity to see and treat others with such loving kindheartedness, nonjudgmental acceptance, and welcoming embrace that it reveals the heart of God. No matter what, no matter where, no matter how life turns or who turns up at the door.

You don't have to be a social analyst to sense the increasing isolation, tribalism, otherizing, fear rhetoric, enemy making, and unwillingness to merely listen to each other in our culture. Wounds cut deep, and lines draw long to separate and exclude. You could argue that it's always been like that and maybe you're right. Even more of a reason to find footing on the one thing that has the power to make whole what has been broken; the one thing that matters most (and always has): be compassionate just as God is compassionate. "God is compassionate, loving kindness," writes Gregory Boyle. "All we're asked to do is to be in the world who God is."[3] Compassion is the one thing most needed in any life, in every context. It translates into any language and speaks every dialect. It's an equal opportunity employer and has a no-eject, no-reject policy. And there is not one among us who does not need someone else to see us with compassionate eyes and then say, "I knew you'd come. God always makes his presence known."

So, *be compassionate just as God is compassionate* is an invitation to a quest, a journey of cultivating compassion-filled lives and leadership. This is not beyond us. Perhaps it's been a while since we've noticed compassion's presence. Maybe it's been trampled upon, or a lot of stuff has been piled on top of it, but it's there. And because it's there within us and among us, we can choose right where we are to cultivate ways of living and leading with compassion. We can decide to join the God of compassion in compassionating a world that can be cruel, hurtful, and divisive, a world aching to know it is loved.

Further, by saying yes to the invitation to cultivate compassion-filled lives, we will find ourselves awakening to conscious contact with God's compassionating presence in all of life. Being compassionate just as God is compassionate relocates us to the center of image-of-God personhood, where we discover the fullness of our humanness. It breaches barriers that divide us from one another. And—for the sake of others and ourselves, communities and churches, our lives and leadership—compassionating the world that God so compassion-*ates* moves us to participate in this surprising (and often disorienting) business of being human that "reveals God and expands God's being."[4]

The degree to which we cultivate compassion as the primary way of living and leading in the world will decide the measure of human flourishing. It will, as well, determine our collective capacity to create redemptive communities with expanding circles of embrace, of authentic divine and human connection, that alters the trajectory of our life together toward a hope-filled future.

Chapter One

How I Look, Yo?

The quest for compassion-filled living and leading starts here: learning to see one another and ourselves with compassion, the lens through which God sees us all. We begin here primarily because the sum and substance of spirituality and the essence of being human is a growing, deepening, and transforming awareness of mutually inherent belovedness. That is hard won. Mainly, I think, because God does nothing outside the context of relationships, as a mentor once told me.

You could argue that if looking for a foolproof plan to assure every single person of his or her belovedness, surely God could have thought of a better way, especially since pain and messiness come with the territory of interacting with one another and the likelihood that this approach guarantees things will go wrong in all kinds of ways.

Naturally, this creates a tension: awakening to a sense of our belovedness does not happen in a vacuum of isolation but only occurs within the context of the relationships that constitute our lives. And yet, the relationships that form our lives often create a void of painful separation that poses a significant threat to awakening to such a thing. In other words, you can't see someone else's belovedness if you are not at least in the process of recognizing your own; and you can't recognize your own unless someone else sees you as beloved.

We learn to see ourselves by perceiving how others see us. We see others the way we see ourselves. And the way we see ourselves has a profound impact on how we understand the nature of God and our capacity to trust how God relates to us. Since emotional pain is social and awakening to belovedness is communal, we cannot escape the necessary condition of belonging to a community that beholds us in such a way as to reveal our belovedness and reminds us of it when we forget. And we do...forget.

José is laid-back. *Chill,* you might say. Reserved yet reluctant to let anyone get too close too fast. Some of this is personality; some the result of the dehumanizing and violent trauma he's endured and the emotional survival skills he's sharpened because of it. Understandably, he's guarded. Some might perceive this as indifferent. At nineteen years old, he finds himself in the same life situation as many of the kids who grow up in the gang-affected streets of southwest Houston. Lacking education and well familiar with the juvenile justice system, he spent a significant amount of time bouncing around juvenile lockup, then county jail once turning seventeen. With all that, opportunities for "advancement" have been few and far between. Now, with a new baby and baby mama to take care of, he needs a steady job. You'd be right to assume that José is not at the top of employers' must-hire lists. Too much risk, they would say. But a friend with a roofing company cares and is more than willing to give him a shot and pay well. It's a late November day when I pick up José at his apartment for a lunch interview with his potential employer at a local Tex-Mex restaurant. Actually, it's not really an interview. The job is his if he wants it. Roofing is physically demanding work. I have my doubts about whether José—a buck-twenty soaking wet—will jump in after hearing what the job entails. But all goes well. He starts tomorrow.

On the ride back to his apartment, I'm curious about what's going on in his head. "So José, what do you think? You a 100 percent?"

"Yeah, dog! A hundred and ten!" He certainly sounds enthusiastic, confirming his excitement with a fist bump.

"I was thinking you might need work gloves, boots, and maybe some other stuff for work tomorrow. You got any of that at your apartment?"

"No. I ain't got none of that."

Pulling into a store, we gather necessary gear for his new job. As we pass racks of winter coats making a limited appearance in Houston, I'm reminded that the forecast has called for temperatures to drop and for the weather to turn wet and cold. I ask if he has a warm coat. Tugging on a thin, hoodie pullover he's wearing, he says, "I got this!"

"Hmm." I point to the winter coats. "What about any of these? You think they might be a little warmer? Pick whatever you want."

10

For several minutes, we peruse the long coat aisle, which stretches from the front of the store to the back. José runs a hand over the garments, getting a feel for the merchandise. He tries on a few, of varying sizes and colors, and puts each one back. This one is too big. This one is too small. This one is too.... Finally, it looks like he's found one that is just right. Then I catch sight of something that catches me a little off guard. In the middle of the store, oblivious to the crowds walking by, there is José somewhere in his own world, standing almost statuesque. Time seems to have stopped. He arches his back slightly and lifts his head just a little. Slowly moving both palms up and down the front of the coat, feeling the freshness of the fabric, he alternates looking left and right, perhaps checking to see if any of his fellow shoppers have taken notice. As he returns his attention to me, our eyes meet.

"Hey, G. How I look, yo?" he says, posing in front of me, still brushing his hands on the front of the coat. It's apparent I'll be serving as his mirror.

The question hangs in the air between us as something radiates from José I hadn't seen much before. Dignity, pride, and a sense of worth—no, worthiness and amour propre rise from the depths of his brokenness to break the surface of his defended exterior. I'm telling you, he's a sight to behold. Beaming. "José, wow! You look great! You look like that coat was made just for you!" Not a huge smile but a subtle grin cracks the left corner of his mouth while his head nods in agreement. "Yeah. Yeah, G! I like this one."

How I look, yo? Truth be told, it's a question we all wonder about, maybe not out loud in the middle of a crowded store but silently among the competing voices fighting to gain a foothold in our hearts. It's not so much a question of, *Do I look good?* but more like, *Am I OK? Am I adequate? Am I loved? Does anyone notice? Does anyone care?*

As much as we pretend otherwise or prefer it not be the case, *How I look, yo?* is a question that requires someone else to answer for us. Standing in front of a mirror to ask and answer it for yourself, well, it loses a little something.

Social psychologist Charles Cooley theorized in his concept of the looking-glass self that how we see and feel about ourselves is primarily determined by how we perceive the way others see and feel about us.[1] Especially early in our development, regardless of words we hear spoken, more

11

than what we may think in our heads, there exists a gut feeling within the heart of the personal operating system that intuits, positively and negatively, how we are viewed by others close to us and by those sharing the communities in which we live.

So, for example, if I *feel* that I'm seen by others as wanted, a gift, someone who matters, and a person to be celebrated, it's likely I will begin to behave out of a grounded sense of worth and dignity, living with self-confidence and a hopeful view of the world. If, however, I get the sense that others see me as worthless and unwanted, less than or undeserving, I will likely learn to believe that about myself and live with a heavy dose of shame coupled with a corresponding, paralyzing sense that I am a nobody. Either way—or more likely a combination of both—how we see ourselves then shapes how we view others and influences our interactions with them. And, I would suggest, how we see ourselves has a profound effect on our gut-level perception of how we feel God truly feels about us. *How I look, yo?* is not just something we ask others; it's a question we seek God to answer as well.

After a worship service several years ago, a woman named Mary approached me crying with her head down. She was living in a transition house trying to get her life back on track after years of drugs, prostitution, and incarceration had beaten her up and beaten her down. The long, arduous journey she had endured was visible in the deep lines that crisscrossed her face, the shame she carried evident by the way her eyes struggled to meet mine. In treatment again, she was trying one more time to engage her painful past and reclaim a hopeful future. Through a flood of tears, she tried to speak her struggle through a trembling voice: "Pastor, I want to pray but I just can't. I'm nothing but a drug addict. Everyone told me I was a waste and they're right. If you knew the things I've done. I don't even know where to begin. I don't know what I would ever say to God. He wouldn't want to hear what I have to say anyway."

"Well, Mary, let me ask you this: If you were to tell me what you would like to say to God, what would that be?"

In broken speech between sobbing heaves, she began, "I'd say...I love you, God. I...need your help, God. I don't want to...be alone anymore. I want...what you want. I want more of you...in my life...in my heart...I want you to forgive me...I want to love you, I want you to love me." At that point, she looked at me for the first time. And with recognition and surprise in her water-filled eyes, she said with a slight giggle, "I just prayed, I just prayed, didn't I!"

"Yeah, Mary, you did. You sure did. And God hears you. God sees you. There has never been a time in your life when God did not love you. There is no expiration date on that. You, my friend, are deeply loved and not alone."

A daughter of God, who somewhere along the way felt that God saw her as a waste, found a grace; this beloved one who learned to hide her face in disgrace felt divine embrace.

I imagine Jesus was seeking an answer to *How I look, yo?* on the day he followed the crowds into the Jordan River to be baptized by a wild man from the hills. Hundreds of eyes watching, river water pouring over his head, I'm guessing he was a little unsure about what lay ahead. As he came out of the water, the answer he heard—and felt—rained over him to soak his soul, like heaven had spilled over its banks onto that little patch of earth to confirm for him and immerse him within God-created identity. "You are my beloved son, chosen and marked by my love, delight of my life!"[2] Not for the first time or the last, Jesus became grounded that day in his divine belovedness. Something that would come in handy throughout the next few years when a genuine sense of himself was at risk of running aground. Something that comes in handy for all of us.

The quest for a compassion-filled life begins by learning to see and be seen by a love that liberates, a kindness that releases us from prisons of pain, and a grace that grounds us in divine belovedness. We all need to know that God sees us as beloved sons and daughters, looked upon with great delight. We all need to be reminded that, yes, in fact, God chooses us and marks us with love. To get there, we need human context, a relational environment that creates a conduit of compassion through which we are seen and empowered to see one another by this kind of love. We need someone else to see us. Genuinely *see* us. We need someone to see more in us than we see in ourselves. To see in us more than has been communicated to us by the haters around us, more than the fears and self-condemnation within us, more than the mistakes we've made. To bear witness to the *imago Dei* we carry. So there remains no doubt we matter, we are in this together, we are loved—and, more importantly, that we are *lovable*—we are mirrors, each of us, called to behold one another with the gaze of compassion. We are created to reflect and reveal each other's built-in divine dignity. Looking upon one another with eyes of compassion allows awareness of inherent sacred worth to rise from the debris pile of whatever has broken our spirit to reveal our loveworthiness. To behold the fundamental belovedness of others is to catch sight of our own.

Jean Vanier calls this the primary characteristic of being human:

> To reveal someone's beauty is to reveal their value by giving them time, attention, and tenderness. To love is not just to do something for them but to reveal to them their own uniqueness, to tell them that they are special and worthy of attention. . . . The belief in the inner beauty of each and every human being is . . . at the heart of being human. As soon as we start selecting and judging people instead of welcoming them as they are—with their sometimes-hidden beauty, as well as their more frequently visible weaknesses—we are reducing life, not fostering it. When we reveal to people our belief in them, their hidden beauty rises to the surface where it may be more clearly seen by all."[3]

Compassion agitates the spirit, activating our attentiveness to treasure buried beneath the surface. It stirs us to "fix our eyes not on what is seen, but on what is unseen."[4] I suspect most of us must learn (or relearn) this kind of seeing. Growing up racialized in 1960s Mississippi, categorized and isolated because of her skin color, was more than difficult; it was traumatic for Shandra. Now in her mid-fifties, she talks about trying to find her way in a world wounded by cultural, political, and socioeconomic divides, in a community overtaken by a storm of anxiety and resulting unwillingness to understand the "other." She remembers the racist place of her youth, which honored hatred and dehumanized human beings who were, in the words of Dr. Martin Luther King Jr., "harried by day and haunted by night by a nagging sense of nobodiness, constantly fighting to be saved from the poison of bitterness."

Trying to survive in a world of violence and embodied cultural shame, she learned to remain invisible both physically and emotionally, fine-tuning self-protective survival tactics, cautious and selective about whom she would let into her life or not. Mostly not.

"I learned to see and not see." Shandra begins telling her story with a view of an unforgotten past only she can see. "If I was walking to school or to the store and I saw you on the street, I would see you and not see you, so I would stay hidden, stay unnoticed. That was the message from my parents and family. *See but don't see,* they said. If I didn't stay hidden from you, if I didn't see you but let you see me, that was trouble. That's just how I was taught to cope. Living like that hurt me real bad, not just then, but as I got older.

"It's taken me a lot to learn not to live like that. A lot of loss. A lot of pain. A lot of fear. A lot of truth. A lot of help from others. A lot of love. But now, yes, now, I *can* see you and let you see me, and life is much better for me."

Everything has beauty but not everyone sees it, someone once said. True enough, I guess. But there are a lot of reasons for not seeing beauty in everything and everyone. Like being trained "to see and not see" because somewhere along the way you got the message loud and clear that to genuinely see others and allow yourself to be seen by them would create a vulnerability that would become a mess of trouble. A disadvantage like that would need to be avoided at all costs. My hunch is, however, that if given the opportunity to choose between a life of self-protective hiding in the shadows and a life opened to see the beauty around us and divine dignity within us, most of us, like Shandra, would choose the latter. At least we would like to.

What if, with a lot of love, a lot of grace, and a lot of help, we could unlearn how we've learned to see and not see by cultivating compassionate catching sight of each other? What if we learned to behold with kindness the more than mere mortals with whom we share the collective space of our lives?

For ninety days in 2010, Serbian-born artist Marina Abramović exhibited her work *The Artist Is Present* at the Museum of Modern Art in New York City. During that three-month period, over 800,000 people came to see it.

Unusual expressions occupy the world of art, but the uniqueness of this exhibit was that it was made of trust, vulnerability, human connection, and some would say divine encounter. For hours each day, six days a week, for ninety days, Abramović, dressed in a bright red gown, sat on a brown, straight-backed, wooden chair. Opposite her was another chair just like it, empty and waiting for someone to occupy it. Strangers lined up by the thousands just for an opportunity to take their place in that simple wooden chair and sit with her in silence. In exchange for their willingness to meet for a moment, Abramović offered each person a few minutes of her undivided attention. She looked softly into each of their eyes, allowed them to stare into hers. No words. No sharing of personal histories. No touch. Just present and attentive, Abramović held each person in an unbroken, conscious gaze of compassion.

"I gazed into the eyes of many people who were carrying such pain inside that I could immediately see it and feel it," Abramović reflected. "I became a mirror for them of their own emotions. One big Hell's Angel with tattoos everywhere stared at me fiercely, but after 10 minutes was collapsing into tears and weeping like a baby."[5]

I'm not suggesting that learning to catch sight of each other, to see you and let you see me with compassion, we need to pull up a couple of chairs and stare at each other until one of us breaks. I am, however, making the observation that when people are willing to wait in a long line for a few moments of undivided attention from a total stranger, that should tell us something about how isolated we feel and how much we all long to be seen and received with compassion. Closing our eyes to the people with whom we share this planet traps us all in a silent suffering that shuts us down, locks us up, and closes us off. If we are willing to enter the vulnerable space of "closing both eyes to see with the other eye" of compassion, we experience something we all long for.[6] We encounter connection, trust, and something of what it means to be human beings assured that someone notices who we are and cares about what it means to be us. We see that despite the fragmentation within us and the barriers between us, we are all, each and every one of us, interconnected in this God-created dignity-and-worth business of being human. And then, if someone notices who we are and cares about what it means to be us, maybe we begin to trust that the God who compassionates our lives notices and cares too. Replying to *How I look, yo?* perhaps we'll even hear the spirit of God whisper in the wellspring of our life, "You look like my love was made just for you."

To the one who beholds, we belong. To belong is to be loved. To be loved, well, it just doesn't get any better than that.

To dig deeper, turn to part 2: "Catching Sight," page 81.

C h a p t e r   T w o

What's It Like to Be You Today?

B eing smart and rich are lucky, but being curious and compassionate will save your ass," Mary Karr told Syracuse University graduates in her 2015 commencement address. "Being curious and compassionate will take you out of your ego and edge your soul towards wonder."[1] Who doesn't need a little ass-saving from time to time? And if being curious and compassionate is all it takes to make life a little more interesting, count me in.

Not only is compassion-filled living and leading cultivated by growing the capacity to see yourself and others through the loving lens of inherent belovedness, but you also nourish compassion by cultivating curiosity. Linking life and leadership to the divine-human narrative of compassion, curiosity has the power to humanize us all. It can break down preconceived ideas or pictures we hold over one another. It connects you to the story of your own life, leads you to empathize with someone else's, and broadens perspective to the boundless and surprising ways in which the God of compassion never ceases writing a narrative of grace on the collective story of our being human together.

"So, Pastor Gregg, what's it like to be *you* today?" Kenny K. greets me in a hallway before a worship service with his user-friendly, exuberant self. No small talk. Just a head-first dive into a question no one had asked me before.

Unlike typical greetings, like how are you, how's it going, or what's up, this would be difficult to brush off with a "fine" or "good" or "same old, same old." No, this greeting would require something more. It was personal. Connective. Authentic. Open. Curious. And, to be honest, disarming. It penetrated my standard self-protective tactics in a way that left me feeling like he had just shown up uninvited at my front door, walked into the kitchen to help himself to some snacks, plopped down on the living room couch, and propped his feet on the coffee table. *Sure, Kenny K.! Come on in!*

"What do you mean, brother?" I try deflecting, knowing full well what he's getting at and not sure I want to go there.

But he's not having it. He puts his hands on my shoulders, positions his face directly in front of mine to make sure there's no escape, and probes again—this time very slowly, to guarantee nothing gets lost in translation: "I mean, I really want to know what's...it...like...to...be...*you, Gregg...TODAY?*" From the emphasis on the last word, I get the hint that he's looking for a current reflection.

Sidebar: Just so you know, I don't do well with SOD moments (Share On Demand). Not that I'm against them. I've used the SOD tactic many times. But personally, SOD catches me flat-footed. It just takes me a bit to switch gears, get out of my head, and into that heart place where I'm a little more in touch with what's really going on with me.

OK, back to the story. People hurry by into the worship service that begins in a matter of minutes, and since I'm the pastor, I'm sort of required to join them. I only have time to give Kenny K. a brief response to what it's like to be me *today*, so settling into an honest-as-I-can, SOD space, I offer a hurried comeback: "Well, I guess to be me *today* feels a little like I'm being pulled in different directions. I'm having a difficult time finding a place where I feel centered, where I can catch my breath, you know? Gotta go, bro. Let's talk more soon." Quick hug. Good talk. Conversation over.

Except the conversation wasn't over. Through the rest of the day and into a toss-and-turn, restless night, that heartfelt question posed by a compassionately curious friend would not stop circulating in my brain. It left me feeling...well, curious. What *is* it like to be me today? Then I thought, what was it like to be me yesterday, and what will it be like to be me tomorrow? How do stories from my past, my hopes for the future—and all the related thoughts, feelings, anxieties, and insecurities that have a way of bubbling up into my present—shape what it's like to be me today?

18

To this day, that wonderfully simple yet complex question sparks conversations for me, sometimes with my wife, sometimes with friends, sometimes with myself in my own head—which, by the way, is not the best conversation partner (just saying). More than a question, it's become a boarding pass for this crooked and meandering journey to understand, accept, and be at peace with the story of who I am, this life I have, and the spirit of God's movement in and through all of it.

What's it like to be you today? A good question; excellent, in fact. And I have a hunch that if you give yourself permission to get curious about how you would answer, you might just find wrapped in those seven words the gift of what it means to be you in the story of your life today. So, before going any further, let me go ahead and ask you:

What's it like to be *you* TODAY?
To see what you see
Hear what you hear
Smell what you smell
Taste what you taste
Touch what you touch
Be touched by what touched you
Long for a touch you didn't get touched by?
What's it like to be you today?
To think what you think
Feel what you feel
Struggle your struggle
Believe your beliefs
Question your questions
Doubt your doubts
Lie your lies
Know what you know
Know what you wish could be unknown?
What's it like to be you today?
To remember your memories
Dream your dreams
Hope your hopes
Laugh your laughter
Hurt your hurts
Cry your tears?

19

What's it like to be you today?
To be sad with your sadness
Glad about your gladness
Mad with your madness?
What's it like to be you today?
To be from where you've come
Go to places you go
Walk the path you know?
What's it like to be you today?

Compassion moves you to get curious about the story of your own life, connecting you to what it's like to be you today, and to how the spirit of God shows up in your life's story line. "In the Hebrew Bible, God is a mystery who comes with a narrative," writes Walter Brueggemann. "So [Yahweh] never characteristically says, 'I am the Lord,' but says, 'I am the Lord that brought you out of the land of Egypt...' You don't get this God without this narrative."[2] This narrative unfolds on the ground of reality, not in the sky of fantasy. It's revealed through the real lives of real people in real time, living in real places with real stories. The same is true for us. You don't get this God removed from the narrative of what it's like to be you. The only way to recognize God is through your story. Spirituality is not a religious abstraction, like, "I believe in God." Period. Rather, it's incarnational narrative, like, "I believe in God... *who met me at the corner of Main and Fifth when I was about to step in front of a metro bus.*" It's "I believe in God... *who spoke to me in a prison cell to tell me that change was possible.*" It's "I believe in God... *who came to me in a community of compassionate people who believed in me when I couldn't believe in myself.*"

Consider just for a second the biographical nature of the biblical narrative. Of course, there are the familiar names like Adam and Eve and Noah; Abraham, Sarah, Isaac, Rebekah, Jacob, Leah, Rachel, and Joseph; Moses, Miriam, Deborah, Esther, Ruth, David, and Bathsheba; Isaiah, Jeremiah, and Amos; Mary, Joseph, and Jesus; Mary Magdalene, Peter, James, John, and Paul. But there are many more names that don't grab headlines or make it into Sunday school curriculum. The biblical narrative is told through the biographical plotlines of men and women like you and me with issues, questions, and crazy families, all of us trying to answer the question of what it's like to be ourselves while wondering whether God is going to help us figure that out.

"All beings are words of God, his music, his art," writes Meister Eckhart. "Sacred books we are, for the infinite camps in our souls."[3] If you want to know where God is, get curious about the sacred book that is *your* life, whatever is written there and whatever the story discloses. Not the life you wish you had—the life you have. As difficult as it may be to accept, and as disappointing as it may seem (believe me, I get it), the life-giving presence of the spirit of God is working in and through the story of your everyday, what you may perceive very dull, often frustrating, at times painful, seriously flawed, wish-you-had-a-do-over life. God comes in the comical and tragic, the known and unknown, the joy and sadness, the pleasure and pain, the faith and fear, the light and darkness, and in the sanity and insanity. Please don't miss the conjoining "and" in all this. No human story is all or nothing. Being human is a both-and blend. There is no up *or* down, twist *or* turn, no heavenly experience *or* hellish event affecting your life that the God of compassion is not curious about. Depending on your current perspective, this can be both comforting and disconcerting. "Where could I go to get away from your spirit? Where could I go to escape your presence?" the psalmist wonders with what I sense is a mixture of reassurance and exasperation.[4]

God is interested, inquiring, and involved. Not that we're aware or for that matter necessarily care, but God desires that one day we will become aware and care. Maybe that's why "the Word became flesh and blood, and moved into the neighborhood," as John introduces the life of Jesus.[5] Jesus engages people amid the ongoing stories of their lives. He shows up at weddings, parties, funerals, and synagogue. Eats, drinks, and tells jokes and stories. He laughs, cries, and gets angry. He challenges religious leaders, plays with children, touches lepers, eats with "sinners," and, moved with compassion-fueled curiosity, expands the circle of God's embrace to include all of us who never thought we would be invited to the table. Jesus is compassionate, yes, just as God is compassionate. And compassion compels him to get curious just as God is curious about the lives people have and moves him meet them there in the vulnerable, messy mixture of their human journey.

What it's like to be you today matters...a lot. In this exact moment, the script of the mystery of God is being written on the pages of your life.

Getting curious about what's written on those pages leads to encountering this compassionately curious God in the story of *your* life.

Cultivating compassion-motivated curiousness leads to meeting the God of compassion in others as well. Although there can be a powerful pull to believe otherwise, just as the mystery of God is being written on the pages of your life, it's also being written on the pages of everyone else's life. What it's like to be you intersects everyone else's what it's like to be them. Compassion stirs you outward beyond your own story to inquire about and empathize with what it's like to be someone else, and try to understand life as they know it. Then, in what may feel like a great surprise, you discover that God joins lives together that otherwise would have remained segregated. A library of life, stories of people touched and changed by the curiosity of compassion, is built one sacred book at a time.

Did you know 385,000 churches dot the American landscape?[6] Not to mention tens of thousands of faith-based nonprofit organizations. In a country deeply wounded by cultural, political, religious, and socioeconomic divides, in communities fragmented by pervasive anxiety, fear, and lack of understanding, I can't help wondering what would happen if each of those 385,000 church congregations took it upon themselves to locate within the dream of being compassionately curious just as God is compassionately curious about people's stories. Hold that thought. Forget entire churches. What would happen if only ten people from each congregation decided to ask someone they've yet to understand, *What's it like to be you today?* By my math, about four million people across the country would receive the gift of another person listening to at least a part of their story. No committee meetings, budget battles, or program paraphernalia to produce, just people with a pulse willing to get a bit curious about someone's life. In the economics of God's compassion, learning what it's like to be her or him might just uncover more of what it's like to be you.

My wife grew up going to a once-thriving congregation in southwest Houston. Her parents joined the church in the late 1950s before the first brick was laid. For years, Gethsemane United Methodist Church was a growing middle-class congregation of white families living the American dream in one of the first master-planned subdivisions in Houston. Schools, shopping—including an air-conditioned mall (a big deal in Houston)—and recreation opportunities framed an idyllic life for thousands of Anglos in Sharpstown. Gethsemane bore the fruit. With a full sanctuary each Sunday morning, a physical plant to handle its plethora of relevant programs for all ages, and land for future expansion, Gethsemane was the kind of success story bishops like to talk about.

But around 1980, for many reasons including an economic downturn, the neighborhood began to change. The church did not. Over the next twenty years or so, the congregation experienced declining attendance, diminishing resources, and fading relevancy in what would become one of the most densely populated, ethnically diverse, multilingual areas of Houston. The members of Gethsemane were surrounded by folks who didn't look like them or talk like them or come from where they had come from. A church of aging, English-speaking white people, relying on the memory of the way it used to be, resisted the reality of the way things were. Even though they struggled to keep the thing afloat, they were determined to keep "those people" out. Of course, this is not an uncommon story. A similar version has been told thousands of times about congregations across the nation, many of which have closed their doors for good. Bunkers of belief spawning a spirituality of suspicion.

Against this backdrop, ninety-year-old decorated World War II veteran Louis Gammon, a member of Gethsemane since the beginning, stands up in the middle of a worship service in 2011 to protest a proposed partnership with a new organization to be birthed out of Gethsemane. The collaboration under consideration was part of a broad vision cast by pastor Justin Coleman, who ably led the way for Gethsemane. By choosing to be part of the community just outside its doors rather than keeping its doors locked—and themselves barricaded in—the church would regain relevance and vibrancy. Charles Rotramel, my friend, colleague, and coconspirator, is speaking to the congregation about partnering in a new work with disconnected youth in southwest Houston called Houston reVision. He talks about the kids living in run-down, gang-affected neighborhoods and apartment complexes close to the church, most of them caught in the juvenile justice system. He doesn't have to say what everyone in the church knows—every one of the kids is black or brown. The pitch is for Houston reVision and Gethsemane to throw the doors of the church wide open to create a community of compassion for isolated youth who have never experienced such a thing. For kids, desperate to know they are loved and be assured that they belong,

23

nonjudgmental, accepting relationships would be built by caring adults and positive peer experiences would be created, the two ingredients necessary to empower kids on the edge to reenvision hopeful pathways.

Red-faced and spittin' mad, Louis stands on the floor between the pulpit and front pews, interrupts Charles's speech with his over-my-dead-body, get-off-my-lawn dissent: "These kids have stolen from us and damaged our property! We've worked long and hard to keep them out of here. We're not about to let those people in now!"

Pin drop. Talk about awkward. Taken aback and unsure how to respond, Charles counters with the first thought to come to his mind: "Would you be open to just having a conversation with one of these kids?" Surprisingly, Louis agrees. The meeting is set up. Louis meets a fifteen-year-old Latino youth from the neighborhood. They both listen to what it's like to be who they are. Louis's heart is touched, his soul is stirred, and to this day he says to anyone who will listen, "My life was forever changed by that. It was one of the best things that ever happened to me."

Immediately Louis signed on to become one of our first volunteers—and the oldest—as well as one of our most enthusiastic and vocal cheerleaders. Now in his mid-nineties, he still shows up when he can to make sure the kids and their families know there is at least one person who gives a damn about what it's like to be them. And whenever given the opportunity and to anyone who will listen, he tells this story of what it's like to be him. Today there are 600 volunteers and 1,100 youth curious about what it's like to be one another, growing together in an expansive compassionate community called Houston reVision still based at Gethsemane Church.

Oh, and because of people like Louis, Justin, and his pastoral successor, David Horton, as well as many other compassionately curious people, Gethsemane has once again become a congregation brimming with life. Only now there is no such thing as "those people." We are all us.[7] It's a church participating in the collective life of the surrounding community. The sanctuary fills each Sunday morning with people worshipping together in Spanish, Swahili, and English. Open to all, it offers relevant programs to empower and encourage women, men, and children of all ages, needs, and backgrounds. The kingdom of God is pictured in the vivid hues of kaleidoscopic human color.

So I wonder what might happen if even one person from each of the 385,000 congregations across the country became willing to get curious and have a conversation with someone or a group of someones they have determined to keep out. What "my life was forever changed" moments would occur if one person were to ask someone they've yet to understand, *What's it like to be you today?* What kind of life would be breathed into churches, communities, and people who could use a gust of the fresh wind of compassion?

"The Broken Truth, and life itself," writes Douglas Wood, "will be mended only when one person meets another—someone from a different place or with a different face or different ways—and sees and hears...herself. Only then will the people know that every person, every being, is important, and that the world was made for each of us. And slowly, as the people met other people different from themselves, they began to see...themselves."[8]

And although this can feel risky, I don't think it takes much. Just a little bit of openness—to locate your body in a different place, suspend preconceived notions and judgments about people different from you, and listen to one another while checking any need to help, advise, fix, teach, or argue—leads to empathetic recognition of and even connection to ourselves in another. One story at a time, life opens more and more to the wideness in God's mercy and to the depth of mutual human flourishing.

By connecting to ourselves in each other's stories, we may even notice that another One has been present all along as a silent partner in the shared experience of what it's like to be us. "It is absolutely crucial, therefore, to keep in constant touch with what is going on in your own life's story," says Frederick Buechner. And it is equally important "to pay close attention to what is going on in the stories of others' lives. If God is present anywhere, it is in those stories that God is present."[9] The power of curiosity links our lives and leadership to the presence of God in the ongoing divine-human story of compassion.

Imagine it: Untold stories now told, hidden stories now held, unvoiced pain now given voice, isolated and alienating stories now borne witness to within the context of a community of compassion that loves what is as it is. Before our very eyes, we see the power stories hold to humanize, dignify, and break down barriers that have prevented us from a mutuality of shared experience.

And then, who knows? Being compassionately curious just as God is compassionately curious may just take you out of your ego and edge your soul toward wonder…and save not only your ass but a bunch of asses along the way.

To dig deeper, turn to part 2: "Getting Curious," page 87.

Chapter   Three

Pain Demands to
Be Felt

W ith an incarcerated father, a mother he never sees, and a step-
father far away in another part of the country, for all intents
and purposes, Marcos has been alone most of his life. Being
alone led to getting into trouble at school; school trouble led to suspensions;
suspensions to alternative education programs (read: school lockup); school
lockup to juvenile detention. Now he spends each day behind bars in a state
facility where no one comes to see him. Gang-labeled by the system, he's
been imprisoned since he was twelve and hasn't stepped foot in a regular
school since elementary. Can you say "school-to-prison pipeline"? Marcos
has struggled with depression and ongoing thoughts of suicide. Now seventeen, serving a multiyear sentence, he's a long way from anywhere or
anyone, facing a long road to freedom.

That being said, Marcos has an engaging personality and is easy to talk
to. Several minutes into our time together, I ask what he likes to do. He
mentions enjoying books.

"Oh, wow. That's great! What do you like to read?"

"Do you know the author John Green? I like reading his books, like
Paper Towns. And you heard of *The Fault in Our Stars?* I read that too." *OK,
didn't see that coming.*

"Oh yeah, I know who that is, and I know *The Fault in Our Stars.*
What's that line about pain at the end of the book? 'That's the thing about
pain...'"

27

Midsentence, he jumps in to finish the thought: "It demands to be felt. Pain demands to be…felt," he says.

"What does that mean to you, Marcos—pain demands to be felt?"

"To me, it means you have to come into your pain. It's easy to shove it down, play like it don't matter. But that makes everything harder. You have to *feeeeel* it, you know? If you feel it, you can get through it."

In the middle of a hellhole, the smell of jail in the air, the truth of being human comes through the hurt of an isolated yet resilient teenager named Marcos, who, by God's grace, is discovering some sense of wholeness in the middle of his brokenness. *Pain demands to be felt.* Indeed.

Grace has a face, pain has a name. Your face, your story. Your pain, your name. There's just no way around it—at least no healthy way. If you're human, you're going to hurt. How you choose to deal with the pain of being human makes all the difference. As a result of getting curious about your life and the lives of others, the quest for compassion-filled living and leading will offer an invitation, a summons of sorts to come into pain—your pain, his pain, her pain, their pain, our shared pain.

The word *compassion* comes from putting two Latin words together: *com* (with, together) and *pati* (to suffer). Literally, compassion is to *suffer with*. It means "to put ourselves in somebody else's shoes, to feel her pain as though it were our own, and to enter generously into his point of view," as Karen Armstrong writes.[1]

In other words, compassion is someone's pain demanding you to feel it with him. You may feel compassion as a stirring to step in her direction, as an aching to act on his behalf, or as a fire in the belly to fight to make an injustice right. In whatever way you may feel it, compassion is much more than sympathy. Compassion closes the distance created by merely *feeling sorry for* someone and compels you to stand with others in solidarity. Not only does compassion move you toward others who are suffering, but compassion also pushes you to be with them in it. Sympathy separates. Compassion connects. It's the pull of pain on your life.

This pull, this fire, this ache, this inner stirring to stand with others in their pain captures the meaning behind the Greek verb used to describe how Jesus was moved to come into people's pain. *Splanchnizomai,* to have compassion, literally means "to cut up the intestines" or "to be moved in the inward parts." It's used to convey deep emotional energy within the most vulnerable core of personhood. "My heart was moved" or "my heart was broken" are other ways to express it. Multiple texts describe Jesus being "moved with compassion" when he encountered people's pain. From within the core of his humanity, he experienced a visceral reaction to suffering, abuse, abandonment, dehumanization, oppression, and injustice. This feeling was so intense, it drove him to come into the pain.

When Jesus sees the crowds of women, men, and children, harassed and helpless, hassled and hung out to dry, he's moved with compassion. He becomes conscious of a labored inner stirring combined with a forceful urge to act on their behalf. Then, asking the disciples to pay attention, Jesus invites them to let the suffering they see move them to welcome compassion's inner alert to come into pain that makes a demand on them to feel it. He wants them to know that when it comes to standing with those who suffer, the harvest is more substantial than they can imagine with fewer laborers than they think.[2]

"Compassion asks us to go where it hurts, to enter into places of pain, to share in brokenness, fear, confusion, and anguish," Henri Nouwen observes. "Compassion challenges us to cry out with those in misery, to mourn with those who are lonely, to weep with those in tears. Compassion requires us to be weak with the weak, vulnerable with the vulnerable, and powerless with the powerless. Compassion means full immersion in the condition of being human."[3]

The Apostle Paul, writing to the suffering Christian community of Philippi, encourages them to fully immerse themselves in the condition of being human by relating to each another in their pain with the same attitude of compassion as Jesus demonstrated in his life. Paul reminds them that Jesus chose not to hide from his own pain or insulate his life from the suffering of others. In humility—and even humiliation—he was able to welcome the wounds of others because he did not turn away from his own, even to the point of suffering the violence and agony of having his body torn apart and his flesh hammered to wooden beams while his heart was broken by betrayal. By coming into pain demanding to be felt, Jesus became human, and the pain of being human became the pathway for the fullness of the divine. To deny his hurt would be to disown himself. To resist his pain would be to reject God's presence.[4]

When it comes to pain as a pathway to connect personhood with divine presence, I wonder if the church forgets what Jesus gets. Certainly not Christian theology as a whole or all people of faith, but within church communities, regardless of denomination, perspectives persist that see pain as a problem at best and a curse at worst, as if God's blessing can be bestowed only upon those who have their spiritual act together. I guess you'd think we would be beyond this by now. But there still remains a false belief that being a "good" Christian somehow exempts a person from hurt or suffering or struggle, and to experience pain must mean that he or she has done something to displease God and, therefore, deserves his or her plight. As if trusting God more guarantees suffering less, Christians are notorious for saying to hurting people things like, "Well, maybe you just need to have a little more faith." Maybe you've heard, as I have, the oft-used phrase "Well, everything happens for a reason"—implying that God or fate or something out there knows the reason you're suffering, and if you could figure that out and make necessary corrections, everything would be OK. Or how about this one: "God never gives us more than we can handle." Really? I've experienced things that I could not handle on my own. I needed help. I can't imagine I'm the only one. Needless to say, sappy spiritual overtures like these are not helpful. Not right.

Spiritual swill spewed over people in pain creates all sorts of problems, which affect the way we think about and relate to God and each other. I don't have space to adequately address it here, but for the sake of anyone who, on top of suffering, has been hit with a spiritual shame trip for the pain he or she is going through, let me just say a few words. First, this kind of toxic God talk is just plain ignorant and a heap of religious rubbish. More than likely it rises from someone else's fear, shame, and insecurity concerning her or his own pain. In the name of bad religion and, unfortunately, in an abusive use of the name of Jesus—aka Man of Sorrows and Suffering Servant—thoughtless "Christian" responses to suffering pile pain on top of pain by shaming, blaming, and alienating those who desperately need to be embraced and given a compassionate space to feel their pain—and be in the company of others who feel it with them without trying to explain it away.

When the Sufi poet Rabia al-Basri describes healing from years of physical and sexual abuse, she includes a caveat of misgivings about the possibility of sharing her story with others: "I am always holding a priceless vase in my hands. If you asked me about the deeper truths of the path and I told you the answers, it would be like handing sacred relics to you. But most have their hands tied behind their back; that is, most are not free of events their eyes have seen and their ears have heard and their bodies have felt."[5] Yet being willing to untie our hands and come palms up into pain that demands to be felt leads to deeper truths of compassion's movement to bind us together by joining us in the pain.

Second, pain is not a problem for God. "Who among those who have read the Gospels," Origen wrote, "does not know that Christ made all human suffering his own?" In Christian theology and identity, we recognize Jesus by his wounds. "Put your finger here. Look at my hands," Jesus says to Thomas, who, by being brave enough to acknowledge the trauma of seeing his friend—and his hope—put to death, becomes more like the father of faith than the son of doubt. "Put your hand into my side."

Jesus welcomes Thomas to a place of trust by inviting him to touch his wounds. By touching those wounds, Thomas discovers his own pain touched, which leads to his whispering recognition, "My Lord and my God!"[6] Wounds have words, and sometimes no words. Memories hold hurt, not always with facts, but with powerful, deeply embedded feelings. Scars tell stories, albeit some stories we don't know how to share. Even if those stories are known only to us, they remind us where we've been, what we've been through, with whom we've been wounded, what we've overcome, what remains to work through, and how much it hurts to do so. Pain connects us to who we are... to who others are. And our wounds, open and closed, visible and hidden, can rejoin us to God.

I suppose that's why Jesus chooses both his pain and ours as a good place to meet. When we become willing to realize that God identifies with our deepest hurting, we begin the process of experiencing God to be the source of our innermost healing. Rather than being an insurmountable obstacle to connection with God, pain expands the opening of conscious contact with God. By welcoming pain, you embrace yourself. By embracing yourself in your pain, you welcome God. Trusting God flows from encountering the One who does not or will not deny or reject his own suffering or ours. This God of compassion, whose love meets us in the wounds, promises to bind up the brokenhearted by showing up to *suffer with* those feeling all manner of sorrow, misery, and heartache, who cry out in their discomfort for the least bit of reassurance that someone is paying attention. And somehow, by being present in the pain, God's tender, loving-kindness brings beauty from the ash heap of life.[7] Doing love for one another as God does love—that is, to be compassionate just as God is compassionate—calls you and me to do the same.

Admittedly, making arrangements to travel the path of pain is not something people are eager to sign up for, especially in a culture that seems to condition us to turn away from or deny suffering, or—when confronted with it—distract our attention, blame someone else, accuse God, numb the feelings, or try to figure out a way to fix it as fast as possible so we don't have to face it. Drug companies print money because pain gets buried alive. But it's no secret that unresolved pain is going to come out one way or another, causing more suffering for ourselves and others. "Pain and suffering are a kind of currency passed from hand to hand until they reach someone who receives them but does not pass them on," writes Simone Weil. So rather than avoid and therefore give it permission to come out sideways, squirt all over the place, and make a mess of things (I speak from experience here), we might as well learn to come into it with authenticity, honesty, and compassion.

It's not always easy, however, to come into pain demanding to be felt, especially when you're not responding to your own pain making demands on you to feel it.

Following the news that Herod just murdered his cousin John, Jesus has one of those "Wanna get away?" moments. He gets into a boat to find a quiet space where he can process his pain and grief. His best-laid plan for some alone time goes off the rails, though, when the crowds who have been watching his every move get wind of where he's gone and decide to pursue him.[8]

To his surprise, when the boat sloshes up on land, a mob of hurting, broken, and hungry people have already gathered to greet Jesus, welcoming him ashore with their overwhelming needs and requests for relief. We encounter people like this every day, don't we? The guy on the street corner with a stained and ripped cardboard sign that says, "Hungry, need food. Can you help?" The woman living with depression who can't seem to find her way out of the oppressive darkness that presses in on her life. The teenager with so much internal pain that she reasons that the only relief from the anguish on the inside is to cut her flesh on the outside. The addict caught in what feels like a hopeless cycle of craving and fix. People of the pews who come to church each week seeking to make meaning out of what often feels like a meaningless existence. Men and women, boys and girls of all ages, shapes, and sizes who outwardly communicate "It's all good" while they inwardly, desperately seek to believe in something that will give life a little bit of hope. All of these people and more—in fact, all of us—want relief when we are hurting, broken, and hungry. This is the mob; the thousands who seek Jesus out, their pain demanding that he feel it, hoping he can do something—anything—to help.

How does Jesus respond? Still just at the beginning of processing his own grief, and perhaps rising out of his own sense of pain and loss, he's inwardly moved with compassion to join them, to connect with them. Many sick are healed because Jesus responds to compassion's pull on his life to be present with them in their suffering. Jesus doesn't shove down his own pain, play like it doesn't matter. He *feeeeels* it, you know? Leaning into his pain allows him to join others in theirs.

His twelve disciples are not so accommodating. Later that same day, Jesus walks inland to a place off the beaten track. He goes there to spend the rest of the day. His disciples and a few thousand of his friends decide to accompany him. His quest for respite again thwarted.

Around dinnertime, the disciples have finally had it up to their eyeballs with these people. And now everyone's hungry, including them. So, seeing the hurting, broken, and hungry crowd through the perspective of their own hurting, brokenness, and hunger, not to mention recognizing the lack of resources at their disposal, they decide to let Jesus know what they think: "Look, Jesus. We're out here in the middle of nowhere, it's getting really late, and we could all use something to eat. There's no way we can feed all these people. We barely have enough for ourselves. Why don't you send them away? They can go somewhere else to get some supper."

I've been there. More times than I can count. When the hurt, brokenness, and hunger of others press against my unsettled hurt, brokenness, and hunger, I shrink, close off. Ignore and isolate. Disconnect and exclude. All I want to say is "Send them away! I can't deal with this right now!" Maybe you've been there too.

Of course, that's part of this business of being human, isn't it? All this pain demanding to be felt…well, it's a pain in the neck. It can put us on edge. Your pain demanding to be felt has a way of crashing into my unresolved issues. That collision opens the subconscious cave of buried pain and hidden insecurities. Like a slumbering bat colony awakened at dusk to escape its underground chamber on a frantic search to feed, a horde of hurt surfaces and unleashes into the world. I guess that's why people with more trauma and trouble than we know what to do with have more doors closed on them than opened for them. Stigmatizing and disparaging labels and vilifying entire groups, cultures, or nations become convenient excuses to send them away, throw them out, or lock them up. Being confronted by others' suffering stirs up angst about our own. Being unwilling to acknowledge our own brokenness, whether as individuals or collectively as a society, leaves us susceptible to condemn and ostracize others for theirs. We judge ourselves.

From outside in and inside out, both Jesus and the disciples are chest-deep in what William James once called the "torn-to-pieces-hood" of being human, that sense of feeling "divided, fractured, pulled in a dozen directions…[while yearning] for serenity, for some healing of our own."[9]

The difference is how they choose to deal with their torn-to-pieces-hood. The disciples' troubled, "send them away" attitude stands in direct contrast to Jesus's compassionate engagement with the hurting, broken, and hungry crowd. Whereas the disciples react by shrinking, closing off, and excluding everyone but themselves, Jesus's response is to expand, open up, and include all. To his disciples' feigned concern for the crowd's well-being, fully exposed by their request that Jesus get rid of them, Jesus offers another option. "You know what?" Jesus says. "We're not going to send them away. Instead, you give them something to eat. Show me what you got."

"All we have are five loaves and two fish."

"Bring them to me."

Jesus invites the crowd to sit with one another on the grass, takes the limited supply of loaves and fish, looks up as if to introduce the abundance of heaven to the limitations of earth, and blesses it all. He breaks the bread into pieces and hands all of it out to the disciples, who are still trying to figure out what's going on. He asks them to go into the pain of those they were determined to get rid of just a few minutes ago, look each of them in the eyes, and offer them something to eat. And something happens no one saw coming. As everyone eats little pieces of brokenness, they hand over something of their own brokenness to each other. Somewhere in the neighborhood of 5,000 hurting, broken, and hungry people have their fill of dinner together—with leftovers to spare, just in case anyone needs a to-go box.

No one is sent away. No one is excluded. Everyone's world is expanded. Everyone is welcomed. Everyone is opened up to someone new. Everyone's hurt, everyone's brokenness, everyone's hunger is met by someone else's hurt, someone else's brokenness, someone else's hunger. And they all are filled.

I guess that's what they call a miracle. The ever-widening circle of compassion expands imagination to welcome those who have grown accustomed to being sent away. Compassion comes into the pain that demands to be felt to merely say, "Show me what you have. Bring your pain, your limitations, all your not-enough-ness. We can work with that."

All the broken pieces of our shared life become the raw material God uses to put us all back together again, with more than enough left over to include anyone else who is hurting, broken, and hungry. "There is a brokenness out of which comes the unbroken," writes Rashani Réa, "a shatteredness out of which blooms the unshatterable.... There is a cry deeper than all sound whose serrated edges cut the heart as we break open to the place inside which is unbreakable and whole, while learning to sing."[10]

Compassion is the pull of a person's pain on your life. We cultivate compassion by receiving and responding to that pull, which requires the vulnerability and willingness to come into the pain—your pain, his pain, her pain, their pain, our shared pain. Compassion does not solve every problem or fix every situation. It does, however, move us to help carry the burdens that bend the shoulders of someone else. The God who will not break a bruised reed or snuff out a smoldering wick meets both you and the one who hurts in what now becomes a shared wound, a pain felt by both of you. And through the mutual experience of *suffering with*, God moves us toward a healing place where we return to wholeness together.

To dig deeper, turn to part 2: "Coming into the Pain," page 95.

Here. Now. With You.

Compassion is the heart of God. By leaning in to hear the divine heartbeat of love, we discover and love ourselves. Motivated by this love in which we live and move and have our being, we extend ourselves to the world around us. Love embraces. Love moves. Love expands. Love creates. Love sends. We are sent.

To be with each other.

To listen.

To understand.

To give.

To bless.

To pray.

To do justice.

To extend mercy.

To welcome.

To forgive.

To make peace.

To reconcile.

To love the world God so loves.

To love one another just as we are loved.

Sent, in fact, as Jesus was sent.

So, when the "all aboard" announcement invites us to hop on compassion's love train (thank you, O'Jays, for the metaphor), why do some choose to stay on the platform rather than leave the station?

I'm sure there are many reasons, some related to what I've already written. But my hunch is that one explanation relates to compassion's "sending" momentum, as in Jesus's commission in John 20, "As the Father sent me, so I am sending you."[1] To be sent as Jesus was sent means to be moved by the same compassion that moved him. Compassion is a force with both a centripetal and centrifugal movement. In other words, it draws us toward the center of divine love and life (centripetal), and from that center it stirs to send us outward (centrifugal) to a fear-filled, divided world in need of healing and wholeness.

It's important to notice that Jesus spoke his "sending" words to the first followers within the context of a fractured, fragmented, and divided world in need of peace, forgiveness, and reconciliation. It's also important to recognize that when the disciples first heard those words, they were very much afraid to be in that world. They had closed themselves off, removed themselves from society, turned off all the lights, and shut off all contact with the outside world. They were afraid, with good reason, that this broken world would do to them what it did to Jesus.

Jesus came and stood with them in their fear. To help them recenter and catch their breath, he helped them breathe in again the life-giving presence of God and told them to unlock the doors and get out there. Stand in the gaps that create distance in the world God loves and desires to make whole.

By nature, compassion cannot happen from a guarded, invulnerable distance. It sends us to come alongside people who find themselves isolated, separated, segregated, demonized, otherized, and relegated to the margins of peace, justice, and hope.

Compassion challenges spiritual, theological, ideological, racial, personal, and organizational comfort zones. Its movement gets things all stirred up. Whether dividing lines have been drawn from a blueprint of personal, theological, or ecclesial bias or we find ourselves in a church, culture, or society in which structural and systemic lines were drawn long before we arrived, compassion is cultivated by noticing the gaps that marginalize people from each other and God, and going there to close those gaps. Go there, stand there, sit there, listen there, learn there. Be there. Navigate the space between until you occupy with your presence the places of your noticeable absence. Come alongside whoever is on the other side.

Of course, this cuts against the grain of coercive and corrosive cultural narratives that would have us believe that building walls to separate the "us" from the "them" is good for all of us. To be sent as Jesus was sent calls us to larger minds and expansive hearts, stirring us to think God thoughts, to dream God dreams, to love like God loves. Exposed to vulnerability and personal or organizational risk associated with compassion's centrifugal movement outward, some folks—if not many—would rather not go there.

Compassion's orientation to create on-ramps where only lane closures exist stands in stark contrast to the mistaken notion that compassion has no grit, no teeth. It's "campfire kumbaya," one man told me, "everybody getting together and feeling really good about being together, warm and fuzzy and comfortable. Who needs that?"

My first thought was, "Well, I can think of *someone* who might need a little of that. Like right now." I held my tongue.

That said, he did have a point. And while I'm pretty sure "campfire kumbaya" is not the best definition of compassion, it does describe something else.

Scientists have known for a long time about the brain chemical oxytocin, affectionately called the love hormone. During and after childbirth, this neurotransmitter helps with labor, milk production, and bonding with a newborn. When released into the bloodstream, it increases positive attitudes associated with attachment, social bonding, and love. In fact, studies have shown that just getting a whiff of the cuddle chemical seems to create more openness and expand capacity to trust. As campfire kumbaya man observed, it can make you want to get together, feel really good about being together, all warm and fuzzy and comfortable.

When a college student told me he had just met another girl and found himself all of a sudden falling in love...again, I asked, "How do you know it's love?"

"You know, 'cause I've got that woo-woo feeling inside!"

"I do know! Congratulations, my friend."

Oxytocin has that effect. But there's a catch to the chemistry. Dr. Carsten de Dreu's research out of the University of Amsterdam showed limits to the love hormone's power of embrace in the face of a stiff headwind like socialized negative attitudes toward particular people groups. Human subjects dosed with oxytocin were far more likely to favor people who represented their specific "in-group" over an "out-group" for which they carried negative bias. Not surprising, right?

But de Dreu's research pointed to something else: "Oxytocin creates intergroup bias primarily because it motivates in-group favoritism and because it motivates out-group derogation." Moreover, when people huddle together with insiders who share their values and worldview, the levels of oxytocin increase, enhancing loyalty to the tribe.[2]

Comfort zones can cause us to circle the wagons in retreat from outside forces. I heard a political consultant say that for people to unify around a particular candidate or platform, they need a common enemy—someone or something to be against. His observation made it sound like that was a necessary thing to ensure victory, implying that if a common enemy doesn't exist, make one up. As much as I cringed, he was tapping into our susceptibility to surround ourselves with people who think like we think, look like we look, believe as we believe. At the same time, he was pointing to the human bent toward bracketing off those who don't.

Driven by the unchecked ego's preference for comparison, competitiveness, and contrariness, humanity has a flair for divisiveness, a remarkable aptitude for classifying and stereotyping entire groups as good or bad, conservative or liberal, acceptable or unacceptable, friend or enemy, one of us or one of them. For some persons of faith, assessing people as believers or unbelievers, secular or Christian, saved or unsaved is a frequent topic of coffee talk and small group conversations. And with a tendency to think of ourselves a little more highly than we ought, we justly (in our minds) and quite honorably (we reason) evaluate ourselves on the right side of things and those who disagree with us or somehow contradict our perspective to be on the wrong side.[3] Currently in American society, particularly where faith and politics intersect, we are choking on this kind of polarization of "sides," demonizing other groups, sanctifying our own.

We like comfort zones. The challenge to them, however, comes with the territory of compassion's centrifugal sending momentum, especially when comfort zones become holy huddles of self-righteous, judgmental exclusion in the name of the God whose capacity for inclusion and loving action far exceeds our need to remain comfortable.

Jesus issues the call to be compassionate just as God is compassionate within the context of loving your enemies in which he unmasks relational wedges shrewdly disguised as religious faithfulness.[4] Forced to one side are the poor, hungry, suffering, and rejected. On the other side are the rich,

powerful, and self-indulgent, who, by the way, like to congratulate themselves for how good God is to them and how blessed they are to have what
they have (#blessed). Any guesses about which side Jesus stands on and
considers "blessed"?

Within this interaction, Jesus challenges self-interested ways of relating
to others, which set limits on who is worthy of love, kindness, grace, and
equity, and who is not. He exposes the smallness of religiously motivated,
self-centered hostility that goes something like, "If you can't or are unwilling to reciprocate my generosity, if you can't or are unwilling to return
my kindness with well-deserved kudos, if you can't or won't appreciate my
magnanimity, well, you don't deserve any of it."

Jesus responds by saying, "Love your enemies, do good, and give ex-
pecting nothing in return." He goes on to say, if you're looking for a pat on
the back, you have seriously missed the point. Is your view of God really so
small? The most high God does not draw a line in the sand to separate who
is worthy and who is not. If God does not set limits on love's openness, why
should you? Judging and condemning others, kicking them when they're
down while congratulating yourself because you're not, is not the way of
love. This kind of divisive behavior merely exposes your own self-loathing.
Instead, live forgiven, forgive others. Give generously, open and offer yourself. In other words, be compassionate with others and with yourself just as
God is compassionate.

In case you're wondering, Jesus is not offering people a new and im-
proved version of God here. This is not God 2.0. He's jogging the collective
memory of their cultural identity, which is rooted in Yahweh's compassion
for all of humanity. Their identity as a people is grounded in a covenant to
be and become a wholehearted people of Yahweh's whole heart. Never for
the sake of themselves, they are a "kingdom of priests," a human bridge of
Yahweh's compassionate connection to the entire world.[5]

The word in the Hebrew scriptures that captures the unimaginable,
eternal depth and breadth of God's compassionate love is *hesed*, a term vir-
tually untranslatable into English. Efforts to find a suitable equivalent include steadfast love, kindness, loving-kindness, mercy, loyalty, grace, and
compassion, depending on context. *Hesed* is all that and more. You could
string all the English words together into one long hyphenated expression
and still not capture the meaning of *hesed*. Whatever words get used in the

scriptures, the meaning is further amplified by the addition of a phrase like "endures forever." For example, "Because the Lord is good, his loyal love lasts forever; his faithfulness lasts generation after generation."[6]

Hesed describes the indescribable abundance of Yahweh's unwavering devotion and limitless love for humanity. It also applies to how Yahweh calls his people to live generously in a world known for its brutality and enemy making. *Hesed* is known by what *hesed* does. It always involves a tangible action for the sake of others, especially on behalf of those pushed to the edges of protection, power, and justice.

Israel's faith has always been rooted in a trusting relationship with Yahweh, the *hesed* one, who is helper of the fatherless, defender of widows, lover of immigrants, and advocate for justice.[7] Which means that as people of God, they are called to do the same—help, defend, love, and advocate for the most vulnerable, isolated, and powerless among them. After all, this is what the *hesed* one did and continues to do for them.

Hesed sets the foundation for the Ten Commandments and subsequent instructions regarding how Yahweh's people are to treat those on the margins. The impartial *hesed* of Yahweh is to be demonstrated in the unbiased *hesed* actions of his people. "I am loyal and gracious [*hesed*] to the thousandth generation.... Don't mistreat or oppress an immigrant, because you were once immigrants in the land of Egypt. Don't treat any widow or orphan badly. If you do treat them badly and they cry out to me, you can be sure that I'll hear their cry."[8]

When the people of God forget to remember who they are and what life is about, the prophets don't hesitate to remind them. "[Yahweh] has told you, human one, what is good and what the Lord requires from you: to do justice, embrace faithful love [*hesed*], and walk humbly with your God."[9]

Whatever it means to be sent with compassion into a cruel world, it has never implied a call to personal comfort. It is difficult. Testing. Challenging. Because compassion is forged in the fire of relationships, there are times it takes you through a melting and hammering-out process of reexamining the company you keep—as well as the company you keep at arm's length. It aims to close in-group/out-group chasms caused by entrenched attitudes and exclusionary practices by giving a strong push to go where you feel quite uncomfortable.

When compassion sends you outside your comfort zone, it will plop you down in a disorienting position. It's not uncommon to notice inner conflict associated with the way you're accustomed to being in the world. As a person of faith, you may begin to question tightly held beliefs about God and how God shows up in the world. The disparity between who you had thought God to be and the God who is may give rise to some doubt. The shaky scaffolding of inward-looking faith no longer holds up under the pressure of compassion's power to generate a new perspective. The world God loves and invites you to love is not as black-and-white, either-or, who's-in-and-who's-out as you once thought. You see goodness in those labeled by the cultural narrative as "bad," dignity in those dishonored, and God in those deemed godless. What does it mean, after all, that the spirit of God is poured out on all flesh, not just the flesh of those counted among your in-group? You discover you share more in common with those categorized as "other" than you thought. Differences once perceived as a threat now enrich your life. God has a far more expansive reach than you had imagined and is moving you into relationships you never dreamed you would have.

This disruption is necessary to challenge your assumptions of who people are, the circumstances of their lives, and where God is in the midst of that. You begin to see injustices in your community and nation, even feeling anger that moves you to be part of the solution, no longer part of the problem. You find yourself making lifestyle choices as you realize God's kingdom is not about "me" and "mine"; it's about us and ours. Take something like education, for instance. A common tendency is to be concerned only about our own children's education. Compassion, however, broadens our understanding and expands our scope of inclusion so that we're just as concerned about the quality of schools for *all* children, including those exposed to extremely poor standards of learning because of where they live and disparities in socioeconomic levels that create crippling conditions, severely limiting future opportunities for a huge percentage of our population.

Nervousness, confusion, apprehension, and even defensiveness may be side effects of compassion's movement to take you somewhere you've not been or have been reluctant to go before. On top of that, it's possible that family members, friends, work colleagues, and even your church community will not understand the shift they see in you. With this unsettling mix of emotional energy and relational dynamics, temptation to stay put rather than push through to the other side is not abnormal. But if you are willing to press on, to go where you have not gone, stand in the place that makes your knees weak, stomach churn, mouth shut, and ears open, you will be surprised by what you encounter.

In October 2017, two men—enemies, you might say, from vastly different groups—showed up at a white nationalist rally at the University of Florida. Randy Furniss, wearing a white T-shirt covered in swastikas, came to hear a speech to be delivered by Richard Spencer, the man who led a violent, torch-bearing mob of white supremacists through the streets of Charlottesville, Virginia, two months earlier. Aaron Courtney, an African American football coach with dreads, came to protest racial bigotry perpetuated by Spencer and his followers.

Angry protesters around Furniss chanted, "Go home, Nazi scum!" when a man in a green hoodie broke out of the mad rabble, punched him in the face, and darted back into the anonymity of the crowd before Furniss knew what hit him. He stood there stunned, shaken, and bleeding from the mouth.

Something surprising happened then. Courtney, who by that time had been at the protest for about four hours, was about to leave when he noticed the scene unfolding around Furniss. He decided that he'd like to have a little chat with him. Approaching Furniss, he asked, "Why do you hate me? What is it about me? Is it my skin color? My history? My dreadlocks?"

Despite Courtney's repeated attempts to engage, Furniss gave him a silent, dead stare and refused to respond. Frustrated with Furniss's unwillingness to engage, Courtney did the only thing that came to mind. He reached out to ask for a hug. Not once. Not twice. Three times he opened his arms before Furniss finally gave in. And there, standing in the gap of a great divide, hundreds of years old, a white nationalist covered with swastikas and an African American coach with dreads, wrapped their arms around each other.

"Why do you hate me?" Courtney asked once more.

"I don't know" was all Furniss could say.

"And I heard God whisper in my ear, 'You changed his life,'" Courtney said later.[10]

I expect it was something like the whisper of God in his ear that motivated Jesus to spend his life standing in the gaps of great divides.

I suppose Jesus pushed people beyond the narrowness of in-group bias and expanded the circle of compassionate inclusion ever wider because of personal experience.

Conceived in the womb of an unwed teenage mom, something for which she could have very well been stoned to death, Jesus felt religiously motivated self-righteous scorn in utero. Homeless and on a desperate search to find a suitable place for labor and delivery, his parents were turned away at every stop. Mary gave birth to him in a barn.

As an infant, he became a refugee on the run with his family, fleeing a genocidal king on a maniacal killing spree to get rid of every boy under the age of two. King Herod had gotten the twisted idea that one of them would grow up to threaten his throne. He wasn't about to let that happen.

Later, as the family settled, Jesus grew up on the other side of the tracks in the hood called Nazareth, an out-of-the-way ghetto considered so bad that a person's morals were brought into question just being from there. Jesus was no exception.[11] Labeled and categorized, he grew up experiencing his "otherness."

He felt the prejudicial effects of social, economic, religious, and political systems designed to give power to a handful, take it away from everyone else, and exploit the powerless for personal gain. Robbed of dignity, freedom, and identity, the masses were gripped by fear. Rampant physical disease and mental illness were everywhere, with no cure to be found. Suffering and death were around every corner. This was a land of deep darkness where people had given up on God and were quite sure the God they had once heard about had given up on them.

As he got older, Jesus recognized that walls built around us first get blueprinted within us. Hatred, exploitation, and exclusion are matters of the heart. Closed hearts close others off. Puny hearts perpetuate punitive practices. He challenged people to ask God to set them free from their internal prisons of prejudice. Living from the inside out, Jesus offered himself to destroy barriers of hostility, to dismantle bastions of dissension, and to bring near those who were far away. Shalom was his life, so he navigated the space between the gaps to create access for those locked out, welcome for those who had been excluded, and justice for those who needed things to be set right.

He subverted exclusionary socioreligious categorizations of people as acceptable or unacceptable, clean or unclean, righteous or sinner, and drew outrage from faith leaders for doing so. For those weighted down by the religious tyranny of superfluous laws, purity codes, and exploitative practices—and there were many—he colored outside the lines of tradition to introduce them (as well as their oppressors) to God's boundless love and liberty. He took on historically held biases by his words, but more importantly confronted them by going where he wasn't meant to go, standing alongside people he was told not to stand with, and inviting everyone else to stand with them too. His embodied message was to connect the disconnected, touch the untouchable, bless the unblessable, love the unlovable, make whole the fragmented, and restore community to those on the outside looking in. And for those on the inside looking out, he wanted the same things for them too.

The story goes that once he went back to the hood where he was raised. He entered the neighborhood synagogue where everyone knew him. He took the scripture scroll, unrolled it to the prophet Isaiah, and began to read. "The Spirit of the Lord is upon me, because the Lord has anointed me. He has sent me to preach good news to the poor, to proclaim release to the prisoners and recovery of sight to the blind, to liberate the oppressed, and to proclaim the year of the Lord's favor."[12]

He carefully rolled up the scroll and sat down. In the pregnant pause, all eyes were on him, everyone a little perplexed about what Jesus thought he was doing. Breaking the awkward silence, he said, "Today, this scripture has been fulfilled just as you heard it." Mic drop.[13]

At first, everyone was impressed with how well spoken Jesus had become; after all, they reasoned, wasn't he just a carpenter's son? But as Jesus continued to lay out the implications of what he was actually saying, it cut sharply against their ingrained worldview. The mood shifted, and things got uncomfortable—fast. They turned on him, rose up, and ran him out of town. A group pursued him, dragged him to the top of a cliff on the outskirts of town and tried to throw him off the edge. Somehow he wiggled free and got away.[14] Not sure if he ever went back.

For his efforts, he was branded a lawbreaker, called a drunk, and labeled a "sinner," scum of the earth. But he seemed to consider it a privilege to be counted among each and every one of these so-called ne'er-do-wells.

Even some friends and family, thinking he'd become too unhinged for their comfort, called him crazy and attempted an intervention.[15] He didn't seem to mind. Some faith leaders made clear that, by standing with "outsiders," Jesus would never be an "insider." His invitation to the God club was withdrawn. He didn't seem to mind.

When he was born, Jesus was also called Immanuel, literally "God with us." It was a name connected to Yahweh's redemptive history, and it foreshadowed the life he would lead. "Immanuel" joined his life to the ancient truth that Yahweh was always with and would never forsake him or humanity.[16]

At every step of the journey, he identified with people who knew all too well the rejection of being driven away, turned down, and wedged out. Eventually, when his antagonists had enough, he was arrested on trumped-up charges and subsequently sentenced in a kangaroo court to death by crucifixion. At the end of his life, Jesus-Immanuel-God-with-us heard again the message that was spoken when he first made his way into the world: "There's no place for you here with us."

And yet, even when the death sentence was carried out, compassion moved him outward to be with people in their most profound experiences of separation. They crucified him with two others, Jesus between them.[17] Three men suffering the violent, humiliating, and dehumanizing torture of crucifixion, each feeling "the anguish of God's distance, the bare landscape of abandonment."[18] Jesus-Immanuel-God-with-us bridged the distance between life and death with an expansive vision of hope just on the horizon. Barely able to fill his lungs with enough air, through the blood pooling in his mouth, he struggled to speak again the eternal words of Yahweh's promise to never forsake or abandon him or anyone else: "Today . . . you will be . . . in paradise . . . with me."[19]

Maybe this is why the Immanuel promise of God-with-us weaves through the entire biblical narrative, and why the very last words out of Jesus's mouth in the Gospel of Matthew are "I myself will be with you every day until the end of this present age."[20]

Before "catchin' the chain" to a maximum-security prison nicknamed Burning Hell, a middle-of-nowhere place just about as far removed from hope as you can get, Luis bounced around the child welfare system. With no family and no place to go, he got siloed in the system and labeled "unadoptable." Because he got into a fight with a foster sibling in a placement facility, system policy dictated calling the cops. Luis was handcuffed, whisked away, and sucked into the black hole of the criminal justice system. He had little to no advocacy, and for reasons I still don't understand, a judge sentenced him as an adult and told him Burning Hell would be his home, along with a lot of other fifteen- to seventeen-year-olds doing adult time on the other side of razor wire, concrete, and steel.

To close the gap of profound disconnection these kids experience, a faithful group of volunteers and staff compose reVision's team, which descends into Burning Hell once a month. As volunteers and teenage inmates mix it up around tables by telling stories and devouring the pizzas we've brought into the unit, I throw out a question. "When in your life have you felt most included?"

Kids chime in and say things like "At my birthday party when I was eight."

"When I was on a basketball team at school."

"I remember when my mom said she loved me. That's it for me."

"What about you, Luis?" asks a volunteer named Seth, sitting next to him. "When in your life have you felt most included?"

Luis, abandoned by everyone, a kid who has no one, takes a moment to ponder. He then looks Seth in the eye with complete sincerity and says, as if it should be obvious, "Well... right here... now... with you."

Immanuel.

Right here... now... with you matters. A lot. When people find themselves on the other side of a human divide, they're not asking for a church outreach program; they need a real live person willing to be sent to be with them. A call from deep within some lonely chasm echoes, hoping it might be heard by someone willing to locate in the dislocation, position herself among those doing solitary on some distant societal outpost. Right here, now, with you closes the gap of time, breaks through walls of place or circumstance, and bridges human divides to come alongside those stranded in a relational and/or system-imposed hinterland.

Christian theology calls this kind of thing incarnation—the everywhereness, always hereness, eternal nowness of divine love poured into human vessels. Right here, in human flesh, the divine and human coming together

48

now in this place, God-with-us. Even more, Immanuel is the spirit of God right here, now, within us, and, therefore, among all of us.

God-with-us is God-within-us. Each and every one of us. That's enough to break down the barriers of hatred and hostility dividing us, as the Apostle Paul says.[21] From God's point of view—and hopefully from ours—there is no such thing as "insiders" and "outsiders." We're all inside Immanuel's circle of compassion because the God of compassion is within each of us. Efforts to make exceptions, to somehow marginalize others as God-forsaken, cannot invalidate divine indwelling or constrict compassion's expansive embrace.

Right here...now...with you is the fullest expression of God's compassionating presence, no matter which side of a great divide you're on. Immanuel happened, is happening, and will continue to happen. Compassion's name is Immanuel. Compassion has other names too, like Peter and Prisha, Asif and Amanda, Jaylen and Joanna, Chris and Chin-sun, Micah and Makayla. And when compassion sends a person named Seth from outside the walls to meet a person named Luis inside the walls at a place like Burning Hell, God-with-us-and-within-us happens again...for both. God-within one meets God-within another. Gaps get closed. Walls come down.

I suspect that's because of who Love is, how Love moves, and what Love does. Activated by the cosmic energy of agape, compassion is the only power that can open closed hearts and tear down dividing walls. Divine love animates compassion's sending movement and momentum in the world. It collapses old patterns of thinking controlled by the smallness of me-ness and reorients us to a new, larger order of we-ness. It expands the mind and heart, awakening us to a way of being in the world where "the ruling principle is the Spirit of Love, and the pattern of society is one of compassion," writes Stephen Verney, "people giving to each other what they really are, and accepting what others are, recognizing their differences, and sharing their vulnerability."[22]

Agape-activated compassion extends itself to the exiled, welcomes the wounded, and befriends the friendless. It sets a place at the table for those who never imagined there is an open seat. Having a no-reject, no-eject policy, it facilitates belonging where there is none to create connection for anyone. And it moves through your life and mine to do all of this.

And by the way, one more thing about this agape-activated, moving, creating, expanding, sending, gap-closing compassion. Your address can be a home with a bell, the last place you fell, or a prison called Burning Hell, but since the first time it heard your name, as Hafiz says, "It has been running through the streets trying to find *you*. And several times in the last week, God himself has come to my door—asking me for your address, wanting the beautiful warmth of your heart's fire."[23]

To dig deeper, turn to part 2: "Closing Gaps," page 101.

Chapter Five

F-Bombs, Faith, and Fit

C ompassion is revealed, cultivated, and strengthened in community. It is an intensively relational endeavor, requiring human interaction. It is cultivated precisely where human beings meet each other and thus embark on a journey to make sense of how all the puzzling pieces of being human fit together.

So let's talk church. And why don't we start with this?

My life intersected with Kenny C.'s life several years ago on a spring Saturday night. A mutual friend wanted us to meet. With gray, shoulder-length hair parted down the middle, white beard, heavy-metal-band T-shirt partially covering the fading ink of various tattoos, washed-out jeans, and dark sunglasses (worn indoors), he looked like a founding member of the Grateful Dead.

Kenny C. had an agenda with two questions. Could he start a new Narcotics Anonymous meeting in our church facilities? That was a no-brainer. My answer was an immediate yes.

Next question? After telling me in no uncertain terms that he wasn't into organized religion (no offense) and that he wasn't sure about the whole God thing (with respect), he asked, "Do I have to come to church to do this?"

"Don't worry," I said, "I'm not much into organized religion either (no offense). Plus, we're not very religious around here—and we're not very organized. It's more of a mess, if you want to know the truth, and most of us are trying to figure out this whole God thing, anyway (with respect). So

51

no, you don't have to come to church. You're welcome however you want to be here or not be here."

Within a couple of weeks, the Living Clean meeting was up and running on Saturday nights following the worship service. Before long, it became the largest NA meeting in Houston, providing an entry point and ongoing recovery for hundreds of men and women on a journey to get clean and live clean.

Even though our church was "a church for people who hate church," as we liked to say, mostly made up of folks in recovery trying to get their spiritual bearings, in Kenny C.'s mind it was still a church, and all churches might as well be the same. That meant he didn't want anything to do with it.

Only a few steps down a hallway separated the space of NA's Living Clean from the hall where we held our weekly worship gathering, but for him, it might as well have been a thousand miles through hostile terrain. Nevertheless, one evening, he mustered the courage to make the treacherous trek into enemy territory. He sat near the front where he could keep an eye on me, kept coming back, and never left. Because he kept showing up, we thought he needed something to do, so we put him in charge of the offering. He couldn't believe we would trust an old dope fiend with the cash.

Between our first exchange and his memorial service a few years later, it was my great delight to be Kenny C.'s pastor, friend, and companion. I learned a lot from him, including how f-bombs artfully and seamlessly dropped into conversations about faith and church could erase disingenuous divisions between the profane and sacred.

Like many who had gotten a message from the church that their "badness" had landed them on God's blacklist of irredeemables, by the time we met he had lived most of his life believing he was a lost cause. At some level, he felt that was true, and he was more than happy to play the bad-boy role. Still, there was a deeper motivation, which drove a search to prove that wrong, both to himself and to others.

In one of our first conversations, he let it all out. "I'm loaded down with so much shame and guilt over what I've done that I don't think I'll ever get through it. I've f*cked up anything good that I've ever had except for recovery and my love for addicts. My demons, at times, are more powerful than I am. I've believed for so long that I was so bad, God doesn't have time for me. I'm a hardheaded agnostic who's felt so unwanted by God. I act like I don't care what people think—that's why the hair and shades—but I do care. I don't feel like I fit…anywhere. And even if I feel like I fit somewhere for a while, I'll do something to make sure I don't fit anymore. You love me now? Just wait. I just want to fit somewhere."

He got into the habit of ending almost every chat with, "Whatever you do, Gregg, don't give up on me. Please, don't give up on me. Love you." I suppose for Kenny C., those five words, "Don't give up on me," revealed both the fear and the hope he carried. Convinced his "bad" self was too broken for anyone to hold, he feared people would decide not to stick with him once they got to know him. At the same time, he hoped that there would be—just might be—a someone or group of someones who would not give up on him even when they got to know him. "Don't give up on me" was another way of saying, "Is there such a place where someone like me can fit? Is the love of this God you talk about open enough to include someone as bad as me?" That's a longing not lost on anyone.

"Hey, Gregg, I've been reading the Bible, the part where the disciples are hangin' with Jesus," he said once, all excited. "Man, I gotta tell ya, these guys are f*ckups! I can relate. It made me think, these guys were f*ckups, and I'm a f*ckup. If Jesus was these guys' friend, maybe he could be my friend too."

"Kenny, listen to yourself, man. You're wondering if you could be Jesus's friend. Why don't you ask him? I'm sure he'll say yes. I imagine he's been wondering if you would like to be his friend."

Weeks later, Kenny C. grabbed my arm to pull me away from a group I had been chitchatting with. Whatever was on his mind, it felt urgent. Like a confidential informant about to share classified information, he looked around to make sure no one was listening, cupped his hand over his mouth—I guess just in case any lip-readers were standing around—and said under his breath, "Hey, brother, I need to talk to you. I need to talk to you about…the *b*-word!"

"Come again?"

"You know, the *b*-word, dude! I need to talk to you about the *b*-word!"

No idea what he was getting at, and since most conversations with him had been laced with profanity, I thought maybe he was trying to clean up his language, and a particular b-word presented a significant challenge to his efforts. "Oh, are you talking about the word *'bitch'*?"

"Nah, man, come on!" he said, rolling his eyes, a little frustrated I wasn't picking up on his clue. "Not that. The *other* b-word! I need to talk to you about... *baptism*!"

Finally! Top-secret message received.

It took a while—several months, if I remember right—but it all came full circle one evening at his baptism. Encircled by the church community that had embraced him, as water drenched his long stringy gray hair and streamed down his face to soak his heavy-metal-band T-shirt, the content of our f-bomb charged talks about faith, fit, and friendship shaped what I would say to him in that holy ground moment.

"Kenny C., I baptize you in the name of the Father, Son, and Holy Spirit," I said, holding his face between my palms. "The one to whom you have longed to belong welcomes you. About whether or not you could be Jesus's friend, hear his resounding 'Yes!' to you now. And to Jesus's question to you, 'Hey Kenny, will you be my friend?' this moment will always remind you that you said, 'Yes!' God's yes to you and your yes to God have come together. You have found a fit. A fit has found you."

Even with its issues, and probably because of them, the church at its essence is a unique relational ecosystem of grace in which compassion can be cultivated to thrive. This provides the church a significant opportunity to catalyze compassion's movement in the world. Whether or not the church responds to the opportunity is the question.

When you're a pastor, folks feel free to give you advice from time to time about sermons you should be preaching and about what they think you should do or not do regarding the pastoral role. This is not a bad thing, necessarily. It provides valuable insight on their view of things and sometimes you're able to glean useful information about what you're up against. When this kind of input comes your way, it usually follows a predictable pattern of communication, perhaps learned in some sort of church people school, which I've never been invited to attend. It goes something like this: say something positive, insert the word *"but,"* and follow with well-informed guidance for which your pastor will thank you.

For example, "Hey, preacher, I like what you do but"—here it comes—
"why don't you talk more about sin? We all need to be reminded how bad
we are—that we're sinners. Tell us about hell too. Preach more on that!"

And then there's this: "I hear all this talk about God's love here, which
is great, but what about God's wrath? There are people out there who are
going to feel the wrath of God. You need to tell them *that*. They need to
repent!"

And for good measure, one more sampling: "I've been a longtime
member here and love this church, but I just want you to know you're driv-
ing me away because you've opened the doors to people who don't understand the first thing about being respectful in church!"

Geez! Give me a break, people. For one thing, statements like these
make me twitch. When did house-training become a prerequisite to enter-
ing the church? I think the church's mission statement should be "No shirt,
no shoes, enter the service!"

Second, about the whole repenting-to-avoid-God's-wrath thing, don't
get me started on the blind self-righteousness of such statements. We all got
stank, a friend says. I got stank, you got stank, all God's children got stank.
And to varying degrees of reek, all stank stinks, especially coming off those
who think their stank don't stink.

And third, a turn-or-burn, fire-insurance motive to trust the God who
is love never did much for me. Sounds like an angry parent saying, "You
better do what I say, boy! Do I need to get my belt?" It's a fear-based, gross
misunderstanding of repentance and an ignorant misrepresentation of
God's character. In fact, doesn't the book say something about there being
no fear in love? Isn't it the abundance of God's goodness and kindness that
leads to repentance?[1] Just saying.

If it's my job to tell folks how bad they are, I must've missed the memo.
Most people feel bad enough without an unsolicited reminder from me, or
anyone else, for that matter.

So no. I feel no obligation to tell people how bad or corrupt or evil or
doomed they are. None whatsoever. And I feel really good about that. For
one thing, I don't believe it. Second, it's just not constructive. Nor is it bibli-
cally honest to reinforce condemnation theology about human wretched-
ness and a God so pissed off at us that he can't stand the sight of us. I don't
care how nicely wrapped in fancy John 3:16 packaging it may be, it doesn't

pass the smell test. Besides, dealing with my own issues takes most of my time, anyway.

I've spent a good portion of my life among folks who for many reasons have felt a significant amount of self-doubt—some of it paralyzing—when it comes to their own goodness. And with that has come a deeply held, sometimes debilitating belief in their inherent badness. You can substitute a lot of other words for "bad." Take your pick. Like those Grace had drilled into her from an abusive alcoholic mother: "Just shut up! You're never going to be anything but a drunk just like me!"

Although she never wrote it on any name tag, ever since Grace was a child, embedded in her identity, the name by which she learned to understand herself even into middle age was A Drunk Like Your Mom. Care to venture a guess as to what her life has been like?

Take the example of a ten-year-old boy I met in a church kitchen. Before preaching in the service, I went to get water. Two boys about ten years old crashed through the door, chasing each other and screaming. When they saw me, they hit the brakes, almost leaving skid marks, stood still, and stared at me. They didn't say a word.

"Hey, guys. I'm Gregg. What are your names?"

"My name's Terrance," the bigger kid said, a little out of breath.

"And what's yours?" I asked his sweaty little friend.

"Don't have one."

"Oh? Wow! I don't think I've ever met anyone without a name. So . . . what do people call you when they want to talk with you or get your attention?"

"Asshole."

"Really? Hmm. Well, what name did your mom and dad give you when you were born?"

"Willie. That's my dad's name too. But they just call me asshole."

I wonder how Willie is doing now.

Of course, believing yourself to be corrupted to the core builds resistance to thinking that it could be possible to belong to anything or anyone good. It takes a toll on your capacity to trust yourself, others, and God. Convinced she was beyond the embrace of love, a young woman told me, "For most of my life, I was taught that God and Jesus and church are only for good people. That wasn't me. My question was, 'Is there a God for bad people, for nobodies . . . like me?' I never thought there was."

I remember thinking, how, for Christ's sake, does anyone ever get the impression, from the church no less, that God and Jesus and church are in the condemnation business? What are we doing here? By "we" I mean the church in general and pastors in particular, people like me who are tasked with shaping the communal ethos and facilitating the cultural expression of being people of Christ's good news in a bad-news world. I felt the need to make amends to her right there on the spot and commit to be part of the healing for anyone I've met who has been church-wounded.

Several years ago, my family was in the car on our way to a church event when my son Campbell, who was six at the time, posed this question: "Dad, why does church always have to be about *God*?" His tone was along the lines of, "Ugh, why do I always have to clean my room?"

"What do you want church to be about?" I asked.

"Me, I guess," he said.

"Well, you're honest, I'll give you that."

The conversation made me wonder: Do we convince ourselves that church is about God, when, in fact, it's about something else? Is it OK for church to be about something else? And if church is not about God, what is it about?

From the way church folks talk about it, I get the sense there are many ways of looking at church and, based on perspective, how we expect to participate (or not) in what God is really up to. Let me give you three that seem very common.

First: *Go to church.* People say things like, *Are you going to church today? You want to come to church with me? I wish I didn't have to go to church. I don't ever go to church. I quit going to church years ago.* And a slight variation on the theme: *Don't forget, next week is bring-a-friend-to-church Sunday!*

Seen through this lens, church is located in a particular place. The language of *going to church* indicates a view of church more like an event happening at a scheduled time in a designated location, usually a building of some sort. This is not that big of a deal. We're a mobile society, moving from point A to point B for things like work, school, recreation, dining, sports events, concerts, travel, etc. We go where we need to go; we go where we want to go. Just like most things, church has its place too, externally positioned and separate from our place. We *go* there. The church and all it offers is based where we are not, and if we want what it has, it will require enough motivation to plan ahead or stop whatever we're doing, move from our current location, and go there to get it. If we don't want what the church has, we can just stay put. Because the church's place and our place are not in the same place, we can easily disconnect.

A second way of looking at the church: *Get out of church.* By this, I don't mean something like when a kid's parents keep dragging him to church against his will, so he racks his brain to come up with an excuse to *get out of it.* I'm thinking of this as a form of benefit analysis. Common expressions include:

"I got a lot out of the sermon today."

"The music at church is awesome—I get so much out of that worship dude."

"I'm just not getting anything out of church, so I think I'm gonna look around for another one."

From this standpoint, church is about product. It's an evaluative parallel to the first posture, a combo package of sorts. We *go to church* and then judge whether what we *got out of church* was worth going for in the first place. If we determine the product good or acceptable, we go back for more. If we rate the quality poor, we face some choices: (a) return to further examine whether the product will eventually meet our needs, (b) keep going back but with growing frustration over unmet needs, either keeping dissatisfaction close to the vest or venting to others about it, (c) decide to look elsewhere, hoping we can get something out of another church, or (d) give up.

And a third way of looking at church: *Get fed at church.* Folks say things such as, *Let me ask you, are you getting fed at church? I miss our old pastor; this pastor just doesn't feed me. I don't get fed at my church, but don't get me wrong, I'm not leaving or anything—I'm getting my spiritual food by listening to so-and-so on TV.*

Similar to the second perspective, *get fed at church* views church as a product, only with a biggie-sized side of spiritual pomposity thrown in. For those with this perspective, the job of the pastor is to serve up healthy portions of solid spiritual food each week because, after all, they were weaned off spiritual milk years ago and need someone else to feed them like the spiritually mature Christians they are.

These three ways of looking at church pose significant challenges, especially if, as my son contended, church always has to be about *God*. Each posture is individualistic, in agreement with my son's assessment about what he would like church to be about—"Me, I guess." "My" needs take precedence over communal commitment. To varying degrees of self-focus and self-absorption, all three see church as something designed to serve us. Church exists for personal fulfillment. Church value is based on the extent to which it satisfies individual needs. Church is a commodity.

Go to church, get out of church, and *get fed at church* betray an approach to church co-opted by a culture of consumerism, "which makes a virtue and goal out of accumulation, consumption, and collecting," writes Richard Rohr. "Normally we cannot see this as an unsustainable and unhappy trap because all of our rooms are decorated with this same color. It is the only obvious story line that our children see. 'I produce therefore I am' and 'I consume therefore I am.'"[2]

During a worship service I visited, an energetic and seemingly very happy pastor was excited to greet everyone in the sanctuary. When it came time for the welcome and announcements, he made sure no one missed the point that it would be his honor if we would make this particular place our church home. "So, if you're church shopping today," he said, "I want to let you know a little about what we do here. We sure hope you'll get a lot out of being here this morning and you'll come back next week. And bring a friend with you!"

Wait, the voice inside my head started chirping, *did he just say 'church shopping'? Really? While you're at it, why not throw in a coupon for a few dollars off next week's offering?*

Writing about "I am the way, the truth, and the life,"[3] one of Jesus's lines that has gotten a lot of attention throughout church history, Eugene Peterson goes Old Testament prophet on us:

> Jesus as the truth gets far more attention than Jesus as the way. Jesus as the way is the most frequently evaded metaphor among the Christians with whom I have worked for fifty years as a North American pastor. In the text that Jesus sets before us so clearly and definitively, way comes first. We cannot skip the way of Jesus in our hurry to get the truth of Jesus as he is worshiped and proclaimed. The way of Jesus is the way that we practice and come to understand the truth of Jesus, living Jesus

in our homes and workplaces, with our friends and family. . . . The cultivation of consumer spirituality is the antithesis of a sacrificial, "deny yourself" congregation. A consumer church is an antichrist church. We can't gather a God-fearing, God-worshiping congregation by cultivating a consumer-pleasing, commodity-oriented congregation. When we do, the wheels start falling off the wagon. And they are falling off the wagon. We can't suppress the Jesus way in order to sell the Jesus truth. The Jesus way and the Jesus truth must be congruent. Only when the Jesus way is organically joined with the Jesus truth do we get the Jesus life.[4]

Perhaps the way of Jesus leads to an alternative way of looking at church: *We are church* is a counterperspective to the other views of *going to church*, *getting out of church*, and *getting fed at church*. Shaped by the Jesus way, *we are church* considers questions like, What if church is not located someplace else, separate from who we are, disconnected from where we live, work, and play? What if church is not a product to shop for and a commodity to consume? What if church is not meant to be a personal feeding trough to get our Jesus on? Contrary to experiences with church that many searching people have, what if church is not about any of that? What if church is about God *and* about us, particularly about the ways in which we participate in the things God is about?

Not long after Jesus said, "I am the way, the truth, and the life," his followers weren't called "the church"; they were recognized as "the Way," because their way of living represented and reflected the life of the one they followed.[5] This Way was a way of *being*. This was a Way that expressed what it meant to *be* participants in God's movement to drench the world with such an outrageous amount of love that people might experience becoming fully alive. This, by the way, was one of the reasons Jesus gave for why he had come in the first place.[6]

For followers of the Way, this meant a mutual sharing of their lives with a community of folks also on the way to becoming genuinely human and fully alive. They did not live this way for their own sakes, but for the well-being of a world of searching people who had been robbed of life and love by a thief who had snuck up on them in the middle of the night and ripped them off.

Learning from our predecessors, this Way views church not as a place or product; it sees church as people. It looks at church not as a some*thing*; it believes church is some*one*. More accurately, church is a kaleidoscopic collective of someones on their way to becoming a community that embodies the reality that "the glory of God is human beings fully alive," as church father Irenaeus imagined.

We are church is people, people on the way of being human and becoming fully alive together because this is what makes God do a happy dance. We're not people of perfect ways, but people with family problems, marital difficulties, money issues, health concerns, traumatic experiences, and addictions. Some of us are parents who have no idea what we're doing. Some of us want to become moms and dads but have been unable to do so, and it breaks our hearts. We do daily battle with our own demons, search to find just a glimmer of light in our dark places, and need companions to mend our wounds and sit with us in the dark. We have doubts, fears, and trust issues that drive us to our knees.

With the collective, communal energy of a grace that seems irrational and certainly outside our control, we interface with the rawness and richness of being human. Our community "holds, contains, and bears witness to"[7] the paradoxical conundrums of broken wholeness, painful healing, profane sacredness, unbelieving belief, questioning answers, disorienting orientation. In our life together, we recognize that the eternal qualities of faith, hope, and love abide in the earthly blend of doubt, despair, and fear.

We're a mess, if you want to know the truth. But we are becoming more and more aware that the spirit of God continues to work with purpose in each of our hearts. "And it is wild and beautiful and perfectly in process. To us it seems like a mess, but God sees a perfect pattern emerging and growing and alive."[8] The spirit of authenticity meets us in what is genuine and true, helping us to embrace this riddled reality of being human, to enter this mysterious mix, and, without trying to create a fix, to do our best to facilitate an honest space of grace in which compassion flows into the shared experience of being transparently human together.

So we gladly make room for the coexistence of f-bombs and faith as folks break free from the harassing and debilitating, not to mention misleading, sense of irredeemability to find the fit of love. We're real—or at least on the way to becoming real people. We're learning to be as honest as we know how to be with real challenges, struggles, and bruises amid the real encounters with the one who holds us together in a love so real that it seems surreal. All the more so because this love doesn't seem to want to let us go. We're real people who accept there's a crack in just about everything, and we're coming to realize, well, maybe that's how light gets in.[9]

For us, "it started when God said, 'Light up the darkness!' and our lives filled up with light as we saw and understood God in the face of Christ, all bright and beautiful. We carry around this treasure of God's light in ordinary clay pots of human frailty to show that the awesome power belongs to God and doesn't come from us."[10]

We are church, on a journey to internalize the Jesus way of creative and redemptive love, and then release it into our relationships. We recognize that every person is a carrier of divine DNA, that Christ is in all things and in all people; everything and everyone belong to God—as labels go, that is the only one that matters.

Especially when confronted with difficult circumstances, we choose to keep cultivating compassion and kindness, humility and patience, although we don't fully understand what that means. There's a process, but we forgive people because we've felt in our bones just how much God has forgiven and forgives us.[11]

Not in isolation but together, we seek to be attentive to how God's abundant love and life mix into the ways we are learning to lovingly live. We're learning how we might become a visible expression of the invisible presence of God. We imagine what it looks like in homes, neighborhoods, and cities when that thing in the Lord's Prayer about "thy kingdom come, thy will be done on earth as it is in heaven" gets real.[12]

In this way of *we are church*, we don't identify with institutional, denominational, or corporate terminology. We prefer a relational typology: family of God, household of faith, brothers and sisters, mothers and fathers, sons and daughters, children of God, bride and groom. Jesus says we're friends; that's good too. We're not so much an organization per se, but a living, breathing organism: dynamic not static, open not closed, risk-responsive not risk-allergic, fluid not stagnate. We're a fully alive body of Christ, human housing for the Holy Spirit, which is poured out on all flesh, not just ours.[13]

We are Spirit-soaked, love-possessed human beings, with mortal bodies and broken hearts. So "here…in this here place, we flesh," to use Toni Morrison's words.[14] Together, in Jesus's way of being church, we flesh. Committed to working out what God is working in us, we flesh. Not alone, but with companions who will not give up on us even when we want to give up on ourselves, we flesh. In a community where our bodies gather, where compassion is revealed, cultivated, and strengthened, we flesh.

And together, we begin to discover that "our fears and anger are transformed by God's unconditional love, and we become gentle manifestations of God's boundless compassion," Nouwen teaches us.

> Our lives become compassionate lives because in the way we live and work together, God's compassion becomes present in the midst of a broken world. Here the deepest meaning of the compassionate life reveals itself. By our life together, we become participants in the divine compassion. Solidarity can hardly be an individual accomplishment. It is difficult for us as individuals to enter into the pains and sufferings of our fellow human beings. But in the community gathered in Christ's name, there is an unlimited space into which strangers from different places with very different stories can enter and experience God's compassionate presence. It is a great mystery that compassion often becomes real for people not simply because of the deeds of one hospitable individual but because of an intangible atmosphere resulting from a common life. Certain [communities like this] have a true healing influence that can make both members and their guests feel understood, accepted, cared for, and loved. The kindness of the individual people often seems more a manifestation of this healing environment than the cause of it.[15]

My friend Dawn once told me about a dream her four-year-old son had. Seth woke up one morning and said, "Mom, I had a dream about God!"

"What did God look like?" Mom asked.

"He had on skinny jeans!" Apparently he was a bit obsessed with skinny jeans.

"What did God tell you?"

Seth opened his arms wide and said, "He told me, 'Welcome home!' "

Dawn went on to say that the conversation with her son brought her to tears. For a very long time, she never gave God much thought. In fact, because of her life experiences, Dawn was one of those who are told not to bother thinking about God because God really doesn't think much of them. Nevertheless, the truth breaking through her consciousness was that there had never been a time when God had not thought about her.

"I have to credit this church for giving me a new set of glasses to see that," she said. "And for letting my son's God be one that wears skinny jeans. I can relate to my son's dream. Every week when I show up in this community, if I listen closely when I walk down the hall and ignore all the hustle and bustle, I can sometimes hear for myself that same whisper: 'Welcome home, Dawn. Welcome home.'"

I wonder what would happen if all churches saw their communities as unique relational organisms in and through which compassion might be revealed, cultivated, and strengthened in the shared journey of being human. What mercy would we see, what stories would we tell?

So with the poet Kamand Kojouri, we keep saying, and all who seek this way of being church continue to say with us:

Come, friends.
Come with your grief.
Come with your loss.
Carry all the pieces of your heart
and come sit with us.
Bring your disappointments
and your failures.
Bring your betrayals
and your masks.
We welcome you no matter
where you come from
and what you bring.
Come and join us
at the intersection of
acceptance and forgiveness
where you will find our
house of love.
Bring your empty cups
and we will have a feast.[16]

To dig deeper, turn to part 2: "Church," page 109.

Chapter Six

Would You Like to Pay with Love?

S o, what's the point?" Blood rushed to my head. Heat radiated from my bald spot. My eyes widened, nostrils flared, and I leaned forward.

"You want to repeat that?"

"Understand, I'm just playing devil's advocate here," the reporter added with a smirk and a chuckle. "I thought that might push your buttons."

He was right about that. I can't tell you how many times I've been asked "What's the point?" or some version of it. It seems to be a question asked when the topic concerns the poor and disenfranchised, posed by people who are not.

"So, really, what's the point?" he continued. "Why are you doing this? A lot of folks would say what you all are doing is a waste of time. You're never going to make a difference, so why do it?"

Specifically in question was Houston reVision's work to put a plug in the school-to-prison pipeline and our work with young men and women in our community currently caught in the juvenile justice system or reeling from its effects. But more broadly, the question concerned any person or organization standing with those pushed to the margins.

It's a fair enough question, I suppose. Most folks in this line of work ask themselves from time to time if what they're doing and how they're doing it, and if the amount of time, energy, and heartache involved, make any difference. And not surprisingly, some people not in this line of work want to know why anyone in his or her right mind would do it.

65

We live and work in a competitive, product-oriented, bottom-line world. People expect progress and advancement in everything from personal relationships to education to career opportunities to spiritual growth to their 401(k)s. We're attracted to, driven by, and buy into results. What's the point if you see only a minimal amount of growth—if you see any at all? What's the point if nothing's ever going to change, if the bottom line remains the same? What's the point if there's not much chance for success—if, in the reporter's words, "you're never going to make a difference"?

What's the point? is related to a family of similar questions that attempt to evaluate and assess the mission value of organizations and churches: How effective is your organization? How do you know if your efforts are successful? What metrics do you use to measure growth and change? What are the three-year plan and business model? Church leaders get caught in this endless cycle of metrics and measurements too. How many, how often, and how much become the basis for goal setting and for guiding weekly, monthly, quarterly, and annual reports on whether a congregation, specific programs, and paid staff members are effective. We count heads, count cash, count programs, compare the numbers to previous counts, and then count ourselves successful or not.

When it comes to data that churches or organizations use to determine effectiveness and reward success, we can all count easily quantifiable things. They have a place, I guess, but does counting what's easily countable miss the point? Sociologist William Bruce Cameron was facing this question when he wrote, "It would be nice if all the data which sociologists require could be enumerated because then we could run them through [computers] and draw charts as the economists do. However, not everything that counts can be counted, and not everything that can be counted counts."[1] A maxim that's definitely worth taking into account when making decisions about what matters and what does not.

So back to the question: What's the point? The answer depends on how you might respond to two other questions: What do you count? What ultimately counts? Churches, organizations, and people tend to measure what matters to them. Whatever we choose to count reveals what counts to us. What counts or, in other words, what we value, in turn, influences decisions regarding what we do, shapes how we go about doing it, and, most importantly, affects how we view the people in our sphere of influence with whom we seek to engage and to build relationships.

Having been in many settings that required a lot of counting, some of which I found tedious and meaningless, if not dehumanizing and manipulative, I'm much more concerned now with what cannot be easily counted but counts for something—things qualitative in nature. What is it that ultimately matters, what is filled with meaning, and what holds fundamental significance? What gets us out of bed in the morning, keeps us awake at night, inspires us to dream, leads us to joy unspeakable, and forces us to our knees to call on a power greater than ourselves? What makes our jaws drop, eyes moisten, and hearts thump? What takes you to the end of yourself only to find the beginning of yourself patiently and expectantly waiting there for you? What releases goodness within, which we had not previously realized was even there? What cannot be taken away, no matter what? What connects us to things that always have been and always will be—timeless things, boundless things, eternal things, which break into our lives through what Celtic spirituality calls "thin places," the spaces where heaven and earth come together, where divine presence intersects human experience? If we pay attention to these things, the aperture of awareness widens to reveal a more life-giving way of being who we are and, therefore, more life-giving ways of doing what we do.

Although not easily counted, at least in ways we tend to measure, the point of cultivating compassion-filled lives is that it counts as one of those things that count most. To *be* compassionate just as God is compassionate is an invitation to a way of *being*. Grounded in love, it's a way of living, working, relating, and cultivating a community that lets go of the need to control outcomes. It is not driven by ego-centered, button-pushing questions like "You're never going to make a difference, so why do it?"

A lot of people do a lot of things—many of which go unnoticed—just because the point is that these things matter most. It matters to them. It matters to folks they love. It matters to God. And the question "What's the point?" doesn't really seem to matter to them at all. In fact, the question itself is an exercise is missing the point all together.

Why? Well, because the point is that it matters to walk patiently with someone who has known only trauma, shame, and alienation, so that at some point in the unpredictable future, in a moment very few people know about, she will experience the light of God penetrating the darkness to offer her a way to freedom.

It matters that a young woman scoops rice and beans onto plates carried by homeless men and women, and is so deeply touched by the encounter, tears drop from her face into each spoonful she serves. And it matters when an older one-legged man weathered by the streets notices her tears and is moved to hobble over on rickety crutches to take her by the hand and say, "Thank you. It's people like you who keep old farts like me going."

It matters that two lifelong friends meet over a cup of coffee so one can share the difficult news: "My lung disease has taken a turn for the worse, and I'm in desperate need of a transplant." When her companion offers invaluable assurance that no matter what, she will be by her side, and then adds, "I want to give you a lung, one of mine," well, that means something. Love translates into giving a body part so your friend might live. How do you measure that?

The point is that it matters when those who have known only condemnation feel accepted and loved. It matters when a former gang member weighted down by the burden of being unable to forgive himself has a breakthrough of grace and love that allows him to finally live free even while serving out the rest of his sentence. It matters that returning citizens go back to jails and prisons to bring hope to incarcerated brothers and sisters. It matters that a middle-aged man, once so tormented by depression that he tried to end his life, now dedicates the gift of his life to walk alongside others debilitated by the same experience. I could go on. And so could you.

Jesus seemed to think the only thing that mattered, the only thing that counts, the only point to any of this is loving one another. "Just as I have loved you, so you also must love each other. This is how everyone will know that you are my disciples, when you love each other." He said everything hangs on two things: "You must love the Lord your God with all your heart, with all your being, and with all your mind.... You must love your neighbor as you love yourself."[2] *Everything* hangs on these two things? That's what the man said.

On my way to a meeting in Austin one morning, I got about forty minutes out of town and needed a bathroom. I pulled into a McDonald's just off the interstate, did what I came to do, and went to the counter for a cup of coffee.

"Good *morning!*" said the young lady behind the cash register. She had purple hair covered by a yellow bandana, a shiny little stud pierced to her left nostril, a big smile, and more enthusiasm than I had expected. I'm thinking she was a morning person.

"Would you like to pay with love?" she asked.

"Uhh, I'm sorry, what was that?"

"Would you like to pay with love?"

"Well…yes…I think so," I said, curious about where this was going. "What did you have in mind?"

"You can choose one of three ways to pay with love," she started the spiel. "You can call someone to tell them you love them. You can send a message, like a text message, to tell someone you love them—"

"Oh man," I interrupted. "I left my phone in the truck. What's the third way?"

"You can also give someone a BIG hug!" she said, a BIG emphasis on "big."

As I looked around the Golden Arches Supper Club for someone who might be receptive to a BIG hug, my options were limited. An old trucker sat in a booth to my left. From the looks of it, he'd been on the road for a while, like days. I wasn't feeling it, and I doubt he'd be feeling it either.

So I turned back to my new friend at the register and asked, "What about you? Can I give you a big hug?"

In a split second, she jumped up, slid across the stainless steel counter between the cash registers like a runner stealing third, and landed in front of me with her arms opened wide, ready to embrace. So we did. Right there in McDonald's, we had ourselves a BIG hug.

"Now, you've just paid with love, and you can get anything you want!" she told me.

"Wow, anything I want? OK, give me a second."

I had only wanted coffee, but after hearing I could get anything, suddenly the entire menu on the board above my head was a buffet of possibility. So I decided to get a full breakfast to go with it. And why not? I had just paid with love.

I walked out of Mickey D's thinking, Who would've imagined you could pay with love? I got back on the road a little more hopeful about the human condition and thought, I wonder what would and could happen if we lived our lives paying with love?

Would you like to pay with love? Maybe that question is the best answer to an inquiry like "What's the point?" And it's an excellent launch point to summarize our considerations of compassion. If being human is to be image bearers of God's love, giving and receiving love taps into the love image of God within us. It inspires the imagination to be in the world in the ways God dreams. Because image and imagination are linked together (*image*-ination), the capacity to imagine for yourself flows out of the image you have of yourself. The image you have of yourself determines how you imagine the world and imagine yourself in the world.

Compassionating love connects to God's love image already and always present and, therefore, motivates participation in authentic expressions of personhood. The more compassion becomes the currency of God's love, the more God's life connects to life as we know it. You learn to see and be seen through the lens of sacred worth. You see each place you put your feet and each person you meet as holy ground. You become curious about people and the stories their lives tell. As you no longer deny the suffering you feel, you're able to respond to compassion's pull to come into the pain of others. You notice gaps of human disconnection and become willing to extend yourself outside personal comfort zones to be with people experiencing alienation. You become drawn to stand with people on the margins, widening the circle of compassion so that margins no longer exist. You know this is an intensively relational endeavor, requiring human interaction, so you learn to commit yourself to a community in and through which compassion continues to be revealed, cultivated, and strengthened.

Compassion creates the condition for growth and change. In real time, over the course of time, being embraced without condition by a compassionate community and treated with positive regard and respect opens space within us that allows hope to break free. We become willing to believe life can be different. Compassion inspires us to "live out of our imagination, the future we wish to create, instead of being held hostage by the memory of our past," writes Stephen Covey.[3]

Maybe the only point is that God thinks it critical for us to cultivate compassion-filled lives. Since being compassionate just as God is compassionate is loaded with eternal weight, what does it look like to cultivate compassion by learning to count it? If as individuals or as churches we want to measure something, perhaps together we can change the scorecard to reflect the compassion-filled people we seek to become and the compassion-filled communities we aim to create. If we determine to make the point that compassion counts, then somewhere along the way we will learn to pay attention to what matters most. More and more, we will begin to experience the immeasurability of being loved, loving others, and loving ourselves.

Will things always go according to plan? Will life work out the way we expect? Will everyone in our lives get it and come along for the ride? Will hurt become a thing of the past? Will it do away with all conflict? Will we no longer struggle? Will every question be answered? The answer to each of these question is most assuredly no. When you choose to pay with love, experiencing failure does seem to be an option. More than an option, actually—a reality. But having said that, I think Rohr's observation strikes a bull's-eye: "If your only goal is to love, there is no such thing as failure.... Even, and most especially, failures are another occasion and opportunity to learn and practice love, even toward yourself."[4]

Compassion is the currency God gives to each one of us to ensure we pay with love every chance we get. By choosing to spend it, it's guaranteed that you will incur no service fees, hidden charges, or penalties for insufficient funds. You cannot overdraw on the inexhaustible compassion of God. So why not make a point of cultivating what counts? Go ahead. Take compassion's currency and pay with love. Spend wildly! It's the only thing that matters.

To dig deeper, turn to part 2: "Counting," page 115.

PART TWO |
CONVERSATIONS AND CULTIVATIONS

Chapter Seven

How to Use Part Two

Introduction

To be honest with you, I am not a fan of religious or leadership programs that come in a box complete with everything you need for success. I've tried many over the years, as I'm sure you have. Every program in a box I have purchased and attempted to put into practice, I did so thinking that once unwrapped and implemented, answers to challenges facing me as a pastor would be provided. Every single one of those boxed programs has landed in another box, either in storage or taken to a landfill.

So before you engage in part 2, "Conversations and Cultivations," let me give you several principles that have guided how I have designed what's ahead.

First, context is everything, and each context is different. In my view, to design and package a program that promises success if you will only follow the instructions, and ensures you will become more productive or more spiritual or more whatever, seems disconnected from reality. It takes your humanity out of context and fails to allow for the rich complexity and natural messiness of life. More than that, a one-size-fits-all approach undercuts what's needed in every situation—the patience, perseverance, and compassionate presence to listen, understand, and respond with imagination to what is happening within your particular cultural and communal context.

Second, God does nothing outside the contexts of relationships. What every context has in common is people—women, men, and children from varying backgrounds, ages, languages, personalities, hurts, and hopes, all trying to make sense of this business of being human at the intersection of the shared spaces and places of their lives.

Because God meets us only in a relational context, I am relatively sure that God never thought it a good idea to send a program to compassionate the world. God invites people like you and me with our own sets of issues, imperfections, nagging challenges and unanswered questions to embody the way of compassion for others who carry baggage of their own and embody compassion for us. And we are invited to do this in the exact location where we feel the terra firma pressing up against the soles of our feet.

Third, God is already present in all situations no matter what, no matter where, no matter when, no matter who. Every person carries inherent dignity and worth, regardless of beliefs, religion, gender, sexual orientation, skin color, socioeconomic status, life situation, or, for that matter, awareness of the divine DNA within.

Fourth, growing in the spirituality of the present, which heightens awareness of the presence of the God of compassion, who meets us here and now, will only empower the conversations and cultivations in the following chapters.

Anthony Bloom suggests, "You will find stability at the moment when you discover that God is everywhere, that you do not need to seek God elsewhere, that God is here."[1] Paying attention to what's going on *here* is challenging. It's convenient, if not comfortable, to focus on what is happening "over there" or "back there" and to be distracted by the many challenges, worries, and fears that seem to call for our attention. Having said that, *here* is an invitation. It invites us to return from "over there" or "back there" to this moment. It asks us to take in this place, this space, this person, this feeling, and, yes, even this struggle.

While it's unrealistic to think we can always in every moment be fully present, by returning here, we become increasingly connected to what is happening and who is happening in front of us, within us, and around us. By returning to the present, we discover the God of compassion has been here all along.

Fifth, questions are as important as answers, if not more so. "Be patient toward all that is unsolved in your heart and try to love the questions themselves like locked rooms and like books that are written in a very foreign tongue," writes Rilke in *Letters to a Young Poet*. "Do not now seek the answers, which cannot be given you because you would not be able to live them. And the point is, to live everything. Live the questions now. Perhaps you will then gradually, without noticing it, live along some distant day into the answer."[2] I suppose God's gift is that we find the answers we seek wrapped within the questions we are willing to ask.

So, rather than offer a shake-and-bake, plug-and-play, or paint-by-numbers package for cultivating compassion, my goal here is to catalyze contextual conversations, cultivations, and imagination. I hope you will invite others into this conversation with you—preferably individuals with experiences different from your own. I can't tell you what applications will come out of your interactions with one another. However, I can say that engaging your context with the goal of cultivating compassionate ways of being in the world is a journey worth taking.

Chapter Layout and Group Process

Part 2 is designed as an interactive framework to use within your context to further conversations and cultivations about compassion-filled living. In sequential order, each chapter in part 2 has a parallel in part 1. So, for instance, "Catching Sight" corresponds to "How I Look, Yo?" "Getting Curious" to "What's It Like to Be You Today?" and so on. You will see each chapter laid out in a five-step process.

Recap, Reflect, Respond, Reengage, and Return

RECAP: Synopsis, takeaways, and conversation starters

In this section, I have included a synopsis of the parallel chapter you have just read and provided space for you to write your own thoughts.

Synopsis: A synopsis of the parallel chapter in part 1.

77

My Three Takeaways: Write what you have learned from the chapter.

My Conversation Starters: Write what you would like to talk about with the group. *Note:* In the "Reflect" step of the process (below), you will see "For Further Discussion," under which I have written group questions. These are not intended to replace the questions you or your fellow group members have written—only to provide options you may wish to consider for your conversation.

REFLECT: Experience and reading

During this part of the session, share experiences with the previous week's cultivating-compassion practice and choose your options to reflect as a group on the topic of the particular session.

Last Week's Reengage Experience: Share your experience cultivating compassion (see below for explanation).

This Week's Reading:

Option 1: Use "My Conversation Starters" above. Choose questions group members have offered.

Option 2: Use questions in "For Further Discussion" below.

Option 3: Draw on a combination of both.

For Further Discussion

Here I've offered some questions you may consider for your group conversation.

RESPOND: What have you heard?

Based on the group's conversation, what have you heard that stirred something within you? Are there any steps you would like to consider taking in your life to further cultivate compassion?

REENGAGE: How to cultivate compassion this week

Practices, reflections, and application exercises are included to raise awareness of compassion's movement and to further cultivate it in the days between sessions. Opportunity is given in each session for group members to share experiences and talk about what has been learned. This is an important aspect of the process and will add life to your experience.

RETURN: How to prepare for the next session

Here you are provided a simple checklist to help you prepare to return to the next session.

What materials do you need?

You will need only three things to participate in "Conversations and Cultivations": your book; a journal, notepad, or way to write down your thoughts electronically; and your life.

Chapter Eight

Catching Sight

What keeps us alive, what allows us to endure?
I think it is the hope of loving or being loved.
I heard a fable once about the sun going on a journey to find its source,
and how the moon wept without her lover's warm gaze.
We weep when light does not reach our hearts.
We wither like fields if someone close does not rain their kindness upon us.

—Meister Eckhart

RECAP: How I Look, Yo?

Synopsis

The quest for compassion-filled living and leading begins by cultivating capacity to see and be seen with compassion, the lens through which God sees us all. The sum and substance of spirituality, and the essence of being human, is a growing, deepening, and transforming awareness of our mutual and inherent belovedness. Awareness of mutual and inherent belovedness only happens by compassion moving us to see one another's sacred worth within the context of the relationships that constitute our lives.

My Three Takeaways

As you read the chapter, what stood out to you about how compassion is experienced and cultivated?

1.

2.

3.

My Conversation Starters

After reading this chapter, what would you like to talk about with your group? Write your questions for group conversation below.

1.

2.

3.

REFLECT: Reading

This Week's Reading: How I Look, Yo?
Option 1: Use "My Conversation Starters" above. Choose questions group members have offered.
Option 2: Use questions in "For Further Discussion" below.
Option 3: Draw on a combination of both.

For Further Discussion

1. Who has answered for you the question "How I look, yo?" In other words, who has revealed to you or reminded you of your belovedness? How did that occur?

2. The relational connection we have with others has a profound influence on how we view ourselves. How we see ourselves affects how we understand God and our capacity to trust how God relates to us. How have you seen this in the lives of people you know?

3. As Jesus experienced in his baptism, we all need to know that God sees us as beloved sons and daughters, looked upon with great delight. What experiences have helped or hindered knowing that God sees you as a beloved son or daughter?

4. Think about Shandra's story. Do you identify with her? If so, what part of her experience connects to your own? In what ways are we taught "to see and not see"?

5. "Closing our eyes to the people with whom we share this planet traps us all in a silent suffering that shuts us down, locks us up, and closes us off."

   • How do we close our eyes to others?

   • How have you experienced others closing their eyes to you?

- What specific individuals or groups in our culture constantly experience eyes closing? What about in the church?

6. Compassion is cultivated by unlearning how we've been taught to see and be seen, and by learning or relearning seeing and being seen "by a love that liberates, a kindness that releases us from prisons of pain, and a grace that grounds us in divine belovedness." Jean Vanier suggests that seeing worth and revealing one another's value is key to being human.

- What specific ways of seeing and revealing does he mention?

- What does he mention as hindering it?

- Is there anything else you might add to the list of what helps or hinders compassionate catching sight of each other?

7. If you, your church, or your group began to cultivate compassion by learning to catch sight of each person in your community, what would that look like? How would you begin?

RESPOND: What have you heard?

Based on the group's conversation, what have you heard that stirred something within you? Are there any steps you would like to consider taking in your life to further cultivate compassion by learning to catch sight of others? In your leadership? In your community? If so, write them below.

1.

2.

3.

REENGAGE: How to cultivate compassion this week

Seven Days of Seeking Not and Being Seen by Love

"Your task is not to seek love," says Rumi, "but merely to seek and find all the barriers within yourself that you have built against it."

To further cultivate compassion by learning and relearning to catch sight of mutual dignity and inherent worth, spend the next seven days *seeking not and being seen by love.*

When I'm having difficulty being seen by God's compassionate eyes—largely due to anxiety about all kinds of things, isolating, feeling shame, not loving others or myself—I repeat silently over and over the identity-shaping affirmation Jesus hears spoken over him at his baptism: "You are my son, chosen and marked by my love, delight of my life."

Intentionally repeating this being-seen-with-compassion encouragement just under my breath throughout the day, and as my eyes close at night, the truth of it begins to settle within to quiet my heart. As my resistance lowers to being seen with compassion, I am able to acknowledge what I feel while sensing God in the middle of what I'm feeling. Gradually, the words break through (my anxiety), and I start to notice God's Spirit praying in my spirit the very same words. I can release myself to presence, be pulled out of the whirlpool of shame, and fall into God's flow of love—until the next time.

The spirit of compassion, which never looks away or ceases to move in your life, sees you and speaks the same dignity-defining words over and within you. "You are my daughter (you are my son), chosen and marked by my love, delight of my life!"

With that in mind, giving yourself permission to trust that the God of compassion already sees you as beloved, over the next seven days, do two things to cultivate compassion in your life.

First: Be as intentional as you can about repeating in your mind, "You are my daughter/son, chosen and marked by my love, delight of my life."

Second: At the end of each day, or during a convenient time, reflect on these three daily questions. Write down your responses in a journal, on a notepad, or on your electronic device.

1. What barriers did I notice within me to being seen with God's compassionate affirmation "You are my son/daughter, chosen and marked by my love, delight of my life"?

2. In what ways did I notice myself resisting someone's words of kindness or affirmation?

3. What did I learn today about barriers to love I have built within myself? What did I notice about becoming more attentive to being seen with compassion?

RETURN: How to prepare for the next session

❑ Read chapter 2: "What's It Like to Be You Today?"

❑ Turn to chapter 9: "Getting Curious." Under the Recap section, write thoughts you may have in "My Three Takeaways" and "My Conversation Starters."

❑ Bring what you learned from the *Seeking Not and Being Seen by Love* exercise.

❑ Offer your experiences and thoughts to the group.

❑ Be responsive to what group members share.

Chapter Nine

Getting Curious

Curiosity is the essence of human existence. Who are we? Where are we? Where do we come from? Where are we going? I don't know. I don't have any answers to those questions. I don't know what's over there around the corner. But I want to find out.

—Eugene Cernan

RECAP: What's It Like to Be You Today?

Synopsis

We nourish compassion-filled living by cultivating curiosity. Linking life and leadership to the divine-human narrative of compassion, curiosity has the power to humanize us all, breaking down preconceived ideas or pictures we hold over one another. Compassion moves you to get curious about the story of your own life, about the stories of others to understand life as they know it, and about how the Spirit of God shows up in your life's story line. Cultivating compassion-motivated curiosity leads to meeting the God of compassion in others.

My Three Takeaways

As you read the chapter, what stood out to you about how compassion is experienced and cultivated?

87

1.

2.

3.

My Conversation Starters

After reading this chapter, what would you like to talk about with your group? Write your questions for group conversation below.

1.

2.

3.

REFLECT: Experience and reading

Last Week's Reengage Experience

Share your experience cultivating compassion: *Seeking Not and Being Seen by Love.*

- What five words would you use to describe the experience?

- What did you learn about yourself?

- What part of the assignment challenged you the most?

- What did you learn about your awareness of compassion's movement in your life?

This Week's Reading: What's It Like to Be You Today?

Option 1: Use "My Conversation Starters" above. Choose questions group members have offered.

Option 2: Use questions in "For Further Discussion" below.

Option 3: Draw on a combination of both.

For Further Discussion

1. What was the most helpful part of this chapter for you?

2. What did you find challenging?

3. In your life, who have you been most curious about? What did you want to know?

4. Who has been the most curious about your life? How has that affected you?

5. Compassion moves you to get curious about the story of your own life and the stories of others. Several years ago, I came across a website called 22 Words. The site is no longer up, but for a while it invited you to tell your story in twenty-two words. If

you wanted to go further, you could choose a topic on which to express your thoughts. In the category "Describe your greatest experience," one man wrote: "I am in a hospital. A nurse hands me a screaming baby and I sat there, looking down, and said, 'Hello son.'" Nailed it. Twenty-two words. No more, no less. Take five minutes, put pen to paper, and try to write your life story in twenty-two words. Then share your twenty-two-word life story with group members. *(If your group includes more than seven people, you may want to split up into smaller groups.)*

6. What did you hear in someone's twenty-two-word story that made you curious to know more?

7. "The script of the mystery of God is being written on the pages of your life. Getting curious about what's written on those pages leads to encountering this compassionately curious God in the story of your life." Do you recall experiences when knowing yourself led to encountering God? If so, would you mind sharing that with the group?

8. Talk about the story of Houston reVision and Gethsemane Church. What part of this story resonated with your experience? Imagine your church or community becoming compassionately curious. What might that look like? What issues do you think it might remedy? How do you think it could start?

RESPOND: What have you heard?

Based on the group's conversation, what have you heard that stirred something within you? Are there any steps you would like to consider taking in your life to further cultivate compassion by getting curious? In your leadership? In your community? If so, write them below.

1.

2.

3.

REENGAGE: How to cultivate compassion this week

Seven Conversations in Seven Days

To further cultivate compassion by getting curious about others' stories, spend the next seven days asking and reflecting on the question "What's it like to be you today?"

Identify seven different people to invite to a conversation with you this week. You can invite someone you know well, an acquaintance, or a work colleague. Try choosing at least two or three people who appear to be very different from you. Also, if there's someone with whom you've had conflict or do not get along, consider a conversation with them. You might try having a brief conversation with a person you just happen to run into—say, the cashier at the grocery store ringing up your purchases. Mix it up. Have fun with it.

Ask each person, "What's it like to be you today?"

If this feels awkward, simply say, "I've been reading about compassion with a group of people, and I've been given an assignment this week. I was wondering if we could have a conversation." Your job is to listen well and ask questions as necessary to further understand a person's story.

Have at least one conversation each day.

Journal each day about what you discover. Over the next seven days, block out a few minutes at the end of each day, or at a time convenient for you, to reflect on the following questions. Write down your thoughts in a journal or notepad, or type them into a phone, tablet, or computer (feel free to bullet-point your responses).

1. What did I learn from the conversation that connected the two of us together?

2. Did any part of this person's story challenge my assumptions about his or her life? If so, what were the assumptions and how were they challenged?

3. What did I notice happening within myself and/or between the two of us?

4. Am I aware of any new insight regarding how getting curious about another person's story affects compassion's movement? If so, what?

5. Reflect on the question "What's it like to be me today?" As you journal your thoughts about the question you've asked others, ask yourself the same question. For a guide, refer to "What's it like to be me today?" below.

6. Bring your seven reflections to share with the group at the next session.

RETURN: How to prepare for the next session

❏ Read chapter 3: "Pain Demands to Be Felt."

❏ Turn to chapter 10: "Coming into the Pain." Under the Recap section, write thoughts you may have in "My Three Takeaways" and "My Conversation Starters."

❏ Bring your stories from *Seven Conversations in Seven Days.*

❏ Offer your experiences and thoughts to the group.

❏ Be responsive to what group members share.

What's it like to be me today?
To see what I see
Hear what I hear

Smell what I smell
Taste what I taste
Touch what I touch
Be touched by what touched me
Long for a touch I didn't get touched by?
What's it like to be me today?
To think what I think
Feel what I feel
Struggle my struggle
Believe my beliefs
Question my questions
Doubt my doubts
Lie my lies
Know what I know
Know what I wish could be unknown?
What's it like to be me today?
To remember my memories
Dream my dreams
Hope my hopes
Laugh my laughter
Hurt my hurts
Cry my tears?
What's it like to be me today?
To be sad with my sadness
Glad about my gladness
Mad with my madness?
What's it like to be me today?
To be from where I've come
Go to places I go
Walk the path I know?
What's it like to be me today?

Coming into the Pain

*A defining moment for me happened when I was getting my locks washed,
and my locker's daughter came in one morning,
and she had been hustling all night.
She had sores on her body, and she was just in a state, drugs.
So something said to me, "Ask her, 'Where does it hurt?'"
And I said, "Shelly, where does it hurt?"
Just that simple question unleashed territory in her that she had never shared
with her mother. She talked about having been incested. She talked about
all of the things that had happened to her as a child,
and she literally shared the source of her pain.
I realized, in that moment, listening to her and talking with her,
that I needed a larger way to do this work.*

—*Ruby Sales*

RECAP: Pain Demands to Be Felt

Synopsis

Compassion is the pull of a person's pain on your life. We cultivate compassion by receiving and responding to that pull, which requires the vulnerability and willingness to come into the pain—your pain, his pain, her pain, their pain, our shared pain. To be human is to hurt. How you choose to deal with pain makes all the difference.

Compassion is someone's pain demanding to be felt and your pain demanding to be felt.

While pain is often problematic for people, pain is not a problem for God. Through the mutual experience of coming into the pain, God moves us toward the healing place where we return to wholeness together.

My Three Takeaways

As you read the chapter, what stood out to you about how compassion is experienced and cultivated?

1.

2.

3.

My Conversation Starters

After reading this chapter, what would you like to talk about with your group? Write your questions for group conversation below.

1.

2.

3.

REFLECT: Experience and reading

Last Week's Reengage Experience

Share your experience cultivating compassion: *Seven Conversations in Seven Days.*

- What five words would you use to describe the experience?

- What did you learn about yourself?

- What part of the assignment challenged you the most?

- What did you learn about your awareness of compassion's movement in your life?

This Week's Reading: Pain Demands to Be Felt

Option 1: Use "My Conversation Starters" above. Choose questions group members have offered.

Option 2: Use questions in "For Further Discussion" below.

Option 3: Draw on a combination of both.

For Further Discussion

1. How did this chapter help you better understand how the movement of compassion is felt?

2. Did this chapter give you any clarity on human pain? If so, what are you clearer about after reading it?

3. Did it raise other questions for you? If yes, what are you wondering about?

4. Compassion is someone's pain demanding you to feel it with them. How have you experienced "this pull, this fire, this ache, this inner stirring to stand with others in their pain"?

5. What's the connection between being honest about our own pain and being able to come into the pain of others?

6. How have Christian responses to suffering hindered experiencing compassion's movement to come into the pain?

7. How have Christian responses to suffering aided your response to compassion's movement to come into the pain?

8. Why is pain not a problem for God?

9. "Show me what you have. Bring your pain, your limitations, all your not-enough-ness. We can work with that." Imagine a church or community as a compassionate, welcoming space for people's pain. If it was your responsibility to create a communal culture of welcoming people in pain, what would be your first step?

RESPOND: What have you heard?

Based on the group's conversation, what have you heard that stirred something within you? Are there any steps you would like to consider taking in your life to further cultivate compassion by coming into the pain? In your leadership? In your church or community? If so, write them below.

1.

2.

3.

REENGAGE: How to cultivate compassion this week

To further cultivate compassion by coming into the pain, spend some time this week with the poem "I Had to Seek the Physician" by Kabir.[1] You may want to write your thoughts in a journal. Here are a few suggestions.

Spend a few minutes each day reading the poem. Read it slowly, several times, paying attention to words or phrases stirring in your heart. What nudges you? What catches your attention? What are you drawn to?

Think or meditate on the word or phrase by asking yourself some questions: What is the meaning of this word for you? What is the spirit of God saying to you? Where does this word or phrase intersect your life situation right now? As you ask these questions or others, listen to how your spirit responds.

Respond by asking God questions about what this may mean for your life or how compassion may be moving you.

"I Had to Seek the Physician"

I had to seek the
Physician because of the pain this world
caused
me.
I could not believe what happened when I got there—
I found my
Teacher.
Before I left, he said,
"Up for a little homework, yet?"
"Okay," I replied.

"Well then, try thanking all the people
who have caused
you pain.
They helped you
come to
me."

RETURN: How to prepare for the next session

❏ Read chapter 4: "Here. Now. With You."

❏ Turn to chapter 11: "Closing Gaps." Under the Recap section, write thoughts you may have in "My Three Takeaways" and "My Conversation Starters."

❏ Bring insights you may have gained from spending time with "I Had to Seek the Physician."

❏ Offer your experiences and thoughts to the group.

❏ Be responsive to what group members share.

Closing Gaps

For the measure of our compassion lies not in our service of those on the margins but in our willingness to see ourselves in kinship with them, in mutuality. That's what we want to achieve—this sense of mutuality. Where we obliterate once and for all this illusion that we are separate. No us and them, just us. For there's an idea that's taken root in the world that's at the root of all that's wrong with it. And the idea would be this: that there just might be lives out there that matter less than other lives. How do we stand against that idea?

—Father Gregory Boyle

RECAP: Here. Now. With You.

Synopsis

We cultivate compassion by being moved out of comfort zones to notice and close gaps that marginalize people from each other and God. Compassion's sending movement cuts against the grain of coercive and corrosive cultural narratives that would have us believe that building walls to separate the "us" from the "them" is good for all of us. The incarnation of Immanuel, God-with-us-and-within-us, is the fullest expression of God's compassionating presence to close gaps that divide.

My Three Takeaways

As you read the chapter, what stood out to you about how compassion is experienced and cultivated?

1.

2.

3.

My Conversation Starters

After reading this chapter, what would you like to talk about with your group? Write your questions for group conversation below.

1.

2.

3.

REFLECT: Experience and reading

Last Week's Reengage Experience
Share your experience cultivating compassion: "I Had to Seek the Physician."

- What five words would you use to describe the experience?

- What did you learn about yourself?

- What part of the assignment challenged you the most?

- What did you learn about your awareness to compassion's movement in your life?

This Week's Reading: Here. Now. With You.
Option 1: Use "My Conversation Starters" above. Choose questions group members have offered.
Option 2: Use questions in "For Further Discussion" below.
Option 3: Draw on a combination of both.

For Further Discussion

1. What two or three insights did you gain from reading this chapter? Was there anything you felt you wanted to push back on as you read?

2. What does it mean "to be sent as Jesus was sent"?

3. How have you noticed the effects of the "love hormone" in groups, social circles, or organizations you've been part of?

4. What are some examples of comfort zones and wall building in our society?

5. "When compassion sends you outside your comfort zone, it will plop you down in a disorienting position." Look back at the

common inner conflicts and side effects resulting from compassion's sending movement out of comfort zones. Identify them and discuss.

6. Did anything strike you as you read about Jesus's experience with prejudice, bias, and "wall building," or about his response?

7. Consider this: "Right here, now, with you is the fullest expression of God's compassionating presence, no matter which side of a great divide you're on." What does that mean? What would it mean to embrace its truth?

8. Take turns and give each person the time to speak the following words to another individual in the group while filling in the blank with his or her name: Compassion's name is _____ . After everyone has been included, discuss these questions:

   • What was your gut reaction when compassion's name connected to yours?

   • Any thoughts as to why you had the reaction you did?

9. Think about what it might look like for you, your church, or your group to be responsive to compassion's sending movement to notice and begin to close gaps that marginalize people from each other and from God. What effect do you think it might have?

RESPOND: What have you heard?

Based on the group's conversation, what have you heard that stirred something within you? Are there any steps you would like to consider taking in your life to further cultivate compassion's movement to close gaps? In your leadership? In your church or community? If so, write them below.

1.

2.

3.

REENGAGE: How to cultivate compassion this week

To further cultivate compassion by moving beyond comfort zones to close gaps that divide, take some time this week to complete the following exercise.

My Inventory of Relationships[1]

This exercise is designed to help us see prejudice or bias. By design, you may feel uncomfortable. So it's a good idea to center and remind yourself to be honest as you take inventory of the relationships in your life.

1. Take a sheet of paper. Write down the names of the people listed below:

  - Spouse or partner

  - Children, grandchildren

  - Siblings

  - Cousins, aunts, uncles, other relatives

  - Lifelong friends

  - Work colleagues

  - Neighbors

  - People you attend church with

  - People you work with in other organizations in which you are involved

- People you know at the gym or through hobbies and activities

- People with whom you are familiar at restaurants or businesses you frequent

- People you most often interact with on social media

2. Indicate which names represent "primary relationships" by either writing the word "primary" beside the names or highlighting them in yellow. A primary relationship is defined as one that is close, personal, and sustained over time. The names you have not identified as primary we will call "secondary" relationships.

3. Now that you have identified all of the primary and secondary relationships, look at the list of characterizations below. Circle the names that fit each characterization. If more than one characterization fits a particular name, draw multiple circles around the name. If you do not know, do not draw a circle.

- Different race or ethnicity

- Different socioeconomic class

- Different neighborhood

- Different family makeup

- Different political leaning

- Different physical challenges

- Different mental health challenges

- Different addictions

- Different religion

- Different expression of Christian faith

- Different sexual orientation

4. Count the number of total names on your paper. Count the number of names you have circled as representing different characterizations from yours.

5. Reflect on these questions:

- What do you notice about your primary relationships?

- What do you notice about your secondary relationships—those not indicated as "primary"?

- What might this suggest to you?

- What feelings are stirring within you?

- Would you be willing to expand your primary relationships with those different from you?

- What are some steps you could take to close the gaps between you and those who have different characteristics?

As a way to venture beyond comfort zones, share what you've learned with your group at the next session. Discuss ways in which you can help each other become more intentional in closing gaps of relationship.

RETURN: How to prepare for the next session

- ❏ Read chapter 5: "F-Bombs, Faith, and Fit."

- ❏ Turn to chapter 12: "Church." Under the Recap section, write thoughts you may have in "My Three Takeaways" and "My Conversation Starters."

- ❏ Bring what you've learned from *My Inventory of Relationships.*

- ❏ Offer your experiences and thoughts to the group.

- ❏ Be responsive to what group members share.

C h a p t e r T w e l v e

Church

*We shouldn't seek the ideal community.
It is a question of loving those whom God has set beside us today.
They are signs of God.
We might have chosen different people, perhaps people who were more caring,
cheerful, intelligent and like-minded. But these are the ones God has given us,
the ones he has chosen for us. It is with them that we are called
to create unity and live in covenant.*

—*Jean Vanier*

RECAP: *F-Bombs, Faith, and Fit*

Synopsis

Compassion is revealed, cultivated, and strengthened in community. Because the church at its essence is a unique relational ecosystem of grace in which compassion can thrive, churches are provided a significant opportunity to become catalysts for compassion's movement. Whether churches respond to the opportunity is the question.

My Three Takeaways

As you read the chapter, what stood out to you about how compassion is experienced and cultivated?

1.

2.

3.

My Conversation Starters

After reading this chapter, what would you like to talk about with your group? Write your questions for group conversation below.

1.

2.

3.

REFLECT: Experience and reading

Last Week's Reengage Experience

Share your experience with *My Inventory of Relationships.*

- What five words would you use to describe the experience?

- What did you learn about yourself?

- What part of the assignment challenged you the most?

- What did you learn about your awareness to compassion's movement in your life?

- Discuss ways in which you can help each other become more intentional in closing gaps of relationship.

This Week's Reading: F-Bombs, Faith, and Fit

Option 1: Use "My Conversation Starters" above. Choose questions group members have offered.

Option 2: Use questions in "For Further Discussion" below.

Option 3: Draw on a combination of both.

For Further Discussion

1. What do you most relate to in this chapter?

2. What are three common ways "church folks" have of looking at church?

3. Which of the three common ways resonate with your experience?

4. What's the alternative way? Talk about the characteristics of this way.

5. Have you ever experienced this alternative way of "being church"?

111

6. Imagine: What would happen if churches saw themselves as unique relational organisms in and through which compassion might be revealed, cultivated, and strengthened in the shared journey of being human?

RESPOND: What have you heard?

Based on the group's conversation, what have you heard that stirred something within you? Are there any steps you would like to consider taking in your life? In your leadership? In your community? If so, write them below.

1.

2.

3.

REENGAGE: How to cultivate compassion this week

To further examine cultivating compassion in community, take some time before the next session to put yourself into the following scenario.

You're In Charge

Through a series of circumstances, you have been put in charge of cultivating a compassion-filled church community. Oddly, every single person in that church community has committed wholeheartedly to buy into what you suggest. No one will argue; everyone is on board (I know, it sounds crazy, but just go with it).

Perhaps it has been years since you have stepped foot inside a church. Maybe your church experience has been less than desirable. It could be you've never been involved in any church or that church has been part of your life for as long as you can remember. It doesn't matter. You've been granted this opportunity because this church community values who you are.

But there's a catch: your task is to cultivate and strengthen compassion only by replacing three practices that have hindered compassion within the church with three practices that will help people in this church community experience compassion and become known for it.

Drawing from your experience, from your humanity, and from what you've been discovering about compassion, answer two questions: (1) What three practices are *you* convinced have to go? (2) What three new practices must be put into action?

Spend some time this week writing down your thoughts. At the next session, you'll be given an opportunity to share these with your group as well as give your reasons. And you'll get to hear from others in your group who are doing the same thing.

RETURN: How to prepare for the next session

❏ Read chapter 6: "Would You Like to Pay with Love?"

❏ Turn to chapter 13: "Counting." Under the Recap section, write thoughts you may have in "My Three Takeaways" and "My Conversation Starters."

❏ Bring your responses from the "You're In Charge" scenario.

❏ Offer your experiences and thoughts to the group.

❏ Be responsive to what group members share.

Counting

What I've come to learn is that the world is never saved in grand messianic gestures, but in the simple accumulation of gentle, soft, almost invisible acts of compassion.

—Chris Abani

Compassion is the chief law of human existence.

—Fyodor Dostoevsky

RECAP: *What's the Point?*

Synopsis

We cultivate compassion by recognizing how much it counts and by learning to count it as individuals and as churches. What's the point of living compassion-filled lives? Whatever we choose to count reveals what counts to us. What counts or, in other words, what we value, in turn, influences decisions regarding what we do, shapes how we go about doing it, and, most importantly, affects how we view the people in our sphere of influence with whom we seek to engage and to build relationships.

Although not one of those things can be easily counted, at least in the ways we tend to measure, the point of cultivating compassion-filled lives is that it counts as one of those things that count most. What does it look like to cultivate compassion by learning to count it?

My Three Takeaways

As you read the chapter, what stood out to you about how compassion is experienced and cultivated?

1.

2.

3.

My Conversation Starters

After reading this chapter, what would you like to talk about with your group? Write your questions for group conversation below.

1.

2.

3.

REFLECT: Experience and reading

Last Week's Reengage Experience
Share your experience cultivating compassion from the exercise *You're In Charge.*

- What three practices did you determine have to go?

- What three new practices did you decide must be put in place?

- Adding to your list: After listening to one another, choose one or two more practices to let go and one or two more to put in place. This will give you a maximum total of five for each question. Talk about what you will add to your lists and why.

This Week's Reading: Would You Like to Pay with Love?
Option 1: Use "My Conversation Starters" above. Choose questions group members have offered.
Option 2: Use questions in "For Further Discussion" below.
Option 3: Draw on a combination of both.

For Further Discussion: *Changing the scorecard*
Read the following paragraph from the chapter:
"If as individuals or as churches we want to measure something, perhaps together we can change the scorecard to reflect the compassion-filled people we seek to become and the compassion-filled communities we aim to create. If we determine to make the point that compassion counts, then somewhere along the way we will learn to pay attention to what matters most. More and more, we will begin to experience the immeasurability of being loved, loving others, and loving ourselves."

Consider what you have done in the *You're In Charge* exercise, what you have gained in recognizing how much compassion counts through the course of reading the book, and what you have learned from spending time with one another.

Beyond how "effectiveness" or "success" are typically measured, discuss as a group what you would do to "change the scorecard to reflect the compassion-filled people we seek to become and the compassion-filled communities we aim to create."

1. Specifically, what do you think needs to be measured?

2. How would you measure it to make sure it counts most?

RESPOND: Next steps?

Since this is the last session on the journey through the book, look back on what you have written in this section. Based on the group's conversations, what you've been hearing and reading, and what has been stirring within you, are there any next steps you would like to consider taking in your life to further cultivate compassion?

1.

2.

3.

Are there any next steps you would like to take as a group to continue cultivating compassion together? Talk about that here.

118

Notes

Prologue

1. Stephen Verney, *Water into Wine* (London: Verney Books, 2015), 71.

2. Luke 6:30-36. Cf. Exod 22:27; Deut 4:31; Exod 34:6; Ps 103:8.

3. Gregory Boyle, *Tattoos on the Heart: The Power of Boundless Compassion* (New York: Free Press, 2010), 62.

4. Meister Eckhart, "Expands His Being" in *Love Poems from God: Twelve Sacred Voices from the East and West*, trans. Daniel Ladinsky (New York: Penguin Group, 2002), 112.

1. How I Look, Yo?

1. Charles Horton Cooley, *Human Nature and the Social Order* (New York: Scribner's, 1902), 152.

2. Matt 3:16-17 in Eugene H. Peterson, *The Message Remix: The Bible in Contemporary Language* (Colorado Springs, CO: NavPress, 2006).

3. Jean Vanier, *Becoming Human* (Mahwah, NJ: Paulist Press, 1998), 22–23.

4. 2 Cor 4:18.

5. Sean O'Hagan, "Interview: Marina Abramović," *Guardian*, October 2, 2012, https://www.theguardian.com/artanddesign/2010/oct/03/interview-marina-abramovic-performance-artist; Jim Dwyer, "Confronting a Stranger, for Art," *New York Times*, April 2, 2010, https://www.nytimes.com/2010/04/04/nyregion/04about.html.

6. Coleman Barks, *The Essential Rumi* (New York: HarperCollins, 1995).

2. What's It Like to Be You Today?

1. Mary Karr, *Now Go Out There (and Get Curious)* (New York: Harper Collins, 2016).

2. Peter Block, Walter Brueggemann, and John McKnight, *An Other Kingdom: Departing the Consumer Culture* (Hoboken, NJ: John Wiley & Sons, 2016), 13.

3. Eckhart, "Expands His Being" in *Love Poems from God*, 112.

4. Ps 139:7.

5. John 1:14 in Peterson, *The Message Remix*.

6. Rebecca Randall, "How Many Churches Does America Have? More Than Expected," ChristianityToday.com, September 14, 2017, http://www.christianitytoday.com/news/2017/september/how-many-churches-in-america-us-nones-nondenominational.html.

7. Hat tip of gratitude and appreciation to Father Gregory Boyle and the homeys and staff of Homeboy Industries, who have shaped my life by beating the drum of kinship, reminding anyone and everyone, "There is no us and them, just us."

8. Douglas Wood, *Old Turtle and the Broken Truth* (New York: Scholastic Press, 2003).

9. Frederich Buechner, *Beyond Words: Daily Readings in the ABC's of Faith* (Grand Rapids: Zondervan, 2009), 379.

3. Pain Demands to Be Felt

1. Karen Armstrong, *Twelve Steps to a Compassionate Life* (New York: Anchor Books, 2011), 8.

2. Matt 9:35-38.

3. Donald P. McNeill, Douglas A. Morrison, and Henri J. M. Nouwen, *Compassion: A Reflection on the Christian Life* (New York: Doubleday, 1982), 3–4.

4. See Phil 2:1-11.

5. Rabia al-Basra, "A Vase," in Ladinsky, *Love Poems from God*, 23.

6. John 20:25-28.

7. Isa 61:1-3.

8. See Matt 14:13-21.

9. Ernest Kurtz and Katherine Ketchum, *The Spirituality of Imperfection: Storytelling and the Search for Meaning* (New York: Random House, 1992), 2–3.

10. Rashani Réa, "The Unbroken," Poems by Rashani, http://rashani
.com/arts/poems/poems-by-rashani.

4. Here. Now. With You.

1. John 20:21.

2. Nicholas Wade, "Depth of the Kindness Hormone Appears to Know Some Bounds," *New York Times*, January 10, 2011, http://www.nytimes
.com/2011/01/11/science/11hormone.html.

3. Rom 12:3.

4. See Luke 6:17-42.

5. See Gen 17:1-8; Exod 19:1-6.

6. Ps 100:5.

7. See Pss 10:14; 68:5; Lev 19:34; Isa 62:8.

8. Exod 20:6; 22:21-23. Cf. Deut 10:17-19; 14:29.

9. Mic 6:8.

10. Mary Hui, "A Black Protester Hugged a White Nationalist outside Richard Spencer's Talk. 'Why Do You Hate Me?' He Asked," *Washington Post*, October 20, 2017, https://www.washingtonpost.com/news
/inspired-life/wp/2017/10/20/a-black-protester-hugged-a-white-nationalist
-outside-richard-spencers-talk-why-do-you-hate-me-he-asked.

11. See John 1:46. When Nathaniel, one of his early followers, heard about Jesus for the first time, he snarked, "Can anything from Nazareth be good?"

12. Luke 4:18-19.

13. Luke 4:21.

14. See Luke 4:16-30; Isa 61:1-2. See also Lev 25:10; Pss 102:20, 103:6; Isa 42:7; 49:8; 49:9; 58:6.

15. Mark 3:20-21.

16. For Immanuel/God-with-us, see Matt 1:23; Isa 7:14.

17. John 19:18.

18. Steve Garnaas-Holmes, "Eloi, Eloi, Lama Sabacthani?" Unfolding Light, April 14, 2017, https://www.unfoldinglight.net/reflections
/syynljw75tz8lgd6baht9pcc2gsl89.

19. John 19:18.

20. Matt 28:20.

21. Eph 2:14.

22. Verney, *Water into Wine*, 24.

23. Hafiz, "Several Times in the Last Week," *I Heard God Laughing: Poems of Hope and Joy*, trans. Daniel Ladinsky (New York: Penguin, 1996), 64.

5. F-Bombs, Faith, and Fit

1. Rom 2:4.

2. Richard Rohr, "Enoughness Instead of Never Enough," Center for Action and Contemplation, February 19, 2016, https://cac.org/enoughness-instead-of-never-enough-2016-02-19.

3. John 14:6.

4. Eugene H. Peterson, *The Jesus Way: A Conversation on the Ways That Jesus Is the Way* (Grand Rapids, MI: Wm. B. Eerdmans, 2007), 4, 6–7.

5. See Acts 22:4; cf. Acts 9:2; 19:9, 23.

6. John 10:10.

7. The phrase "holds, contains, and bears witness" is used by Dr. Matthew H. Russell in the forthcoming "Redeeming Narratives in Christian Community."

8. Wm Paul Young, *The Shack* (Newbury Park, CA: Windblown Media, 2007), 138.

9. "There is a crack in everything / That's how the light gets in." Leonard Cohen, "Anthem" on *The Future* (Columbia Records: 1992).

10. 2 Cor 4:6-7.

11. See Col 3:11-13.

12. Matt 6:9-13.

13. 1 Cor 6:19; 12:27.

14. Toni Morrison, *Beloved* (New York: Vintage Books, 2004), 103.

15. McNeill, Morrison, and Nouwen, *Compassion*, 55–56.

16. Kamand Kojouri, "Come Friends," KamandKojouri.com, January 4, 2017, https://kamandkojouri.com/2017/01/04/come-friends.

6. Would You Like to Pay with Love?

1. William Bruce Cameron, *Informal Sociology: A Casual Introduction to Sociological Thinking* (New York: Random House, 1963), 13.

2. John 13:34-35; Matt 22:37-39.

3. Stephen R. Covey, *The 7 Habits of Highly Effective People: Powerful Lessons in Personal Change* (New York: Simon & Schuster, 2004), 394.

4. Richard Rohr, "Not Merely an Era of Change, but a Change of Era,"

Center for Contemplation and Action, January 31, 2016, https://cac.org /not-merely-an-era-of-change-but-a-change-of-era-2016-01-31.

7. How to Use Part Two

1. Quoted in Brian D. McLaren, *Naked Spirituality: A Life with God in 12 Simple Words* (New York: HarperCollins, 2012), 31.

2. Rainer Maria Rilke, *Letters to a Young Poet*, trans. M. D. Herter Norton (New York: W. W. Norton & Co., 1954), Apple iBooks edition.

10. Coming into the Pain

1. Ladinsky, *Love Poems from God*, 229.

11. Closing Gaps

1. Adapted from Bill Mefford's book *The Fig Tree Revolution: Unleashing Local Churches into the Mission of Justice* (Eugene, OR: Cascade Books, 2017), 61–62.

CPSIA information can be obtained
at www.ICGtesting.com
Printed in the USA
LVHW020122300319
612376LV00003B/4/P